THIS COLORING BOOK BELONGS TO :

____

ALLOW YOURSELF TO RELAX AND FOCUS ON THE COLORING.

ENJOY !

IF YOU LOVED THIS COLORING BOOK PLEASE LET US KNOW THAT BY A LOVELY FEEDBACK

COLOR TEST PAGE

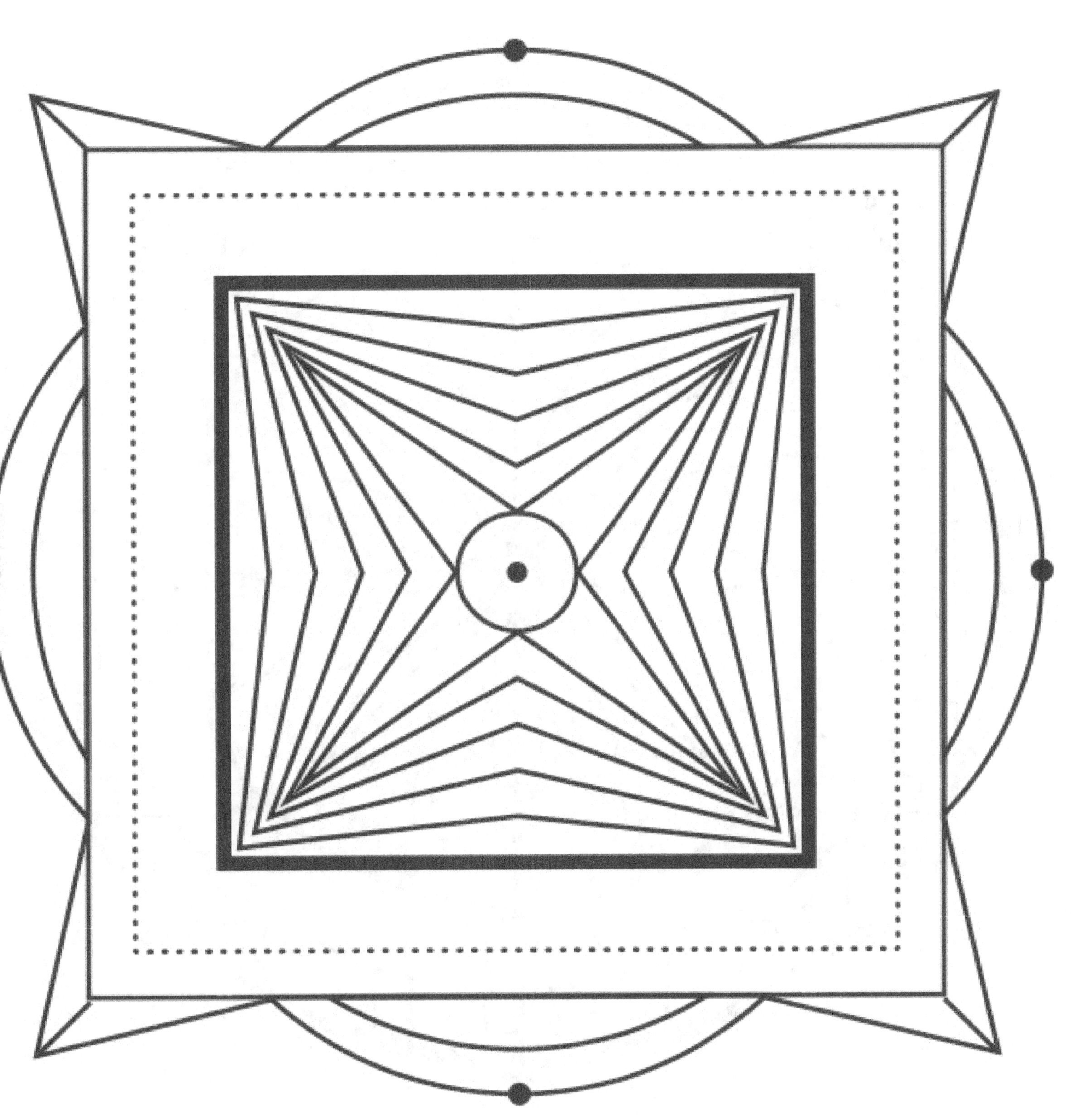

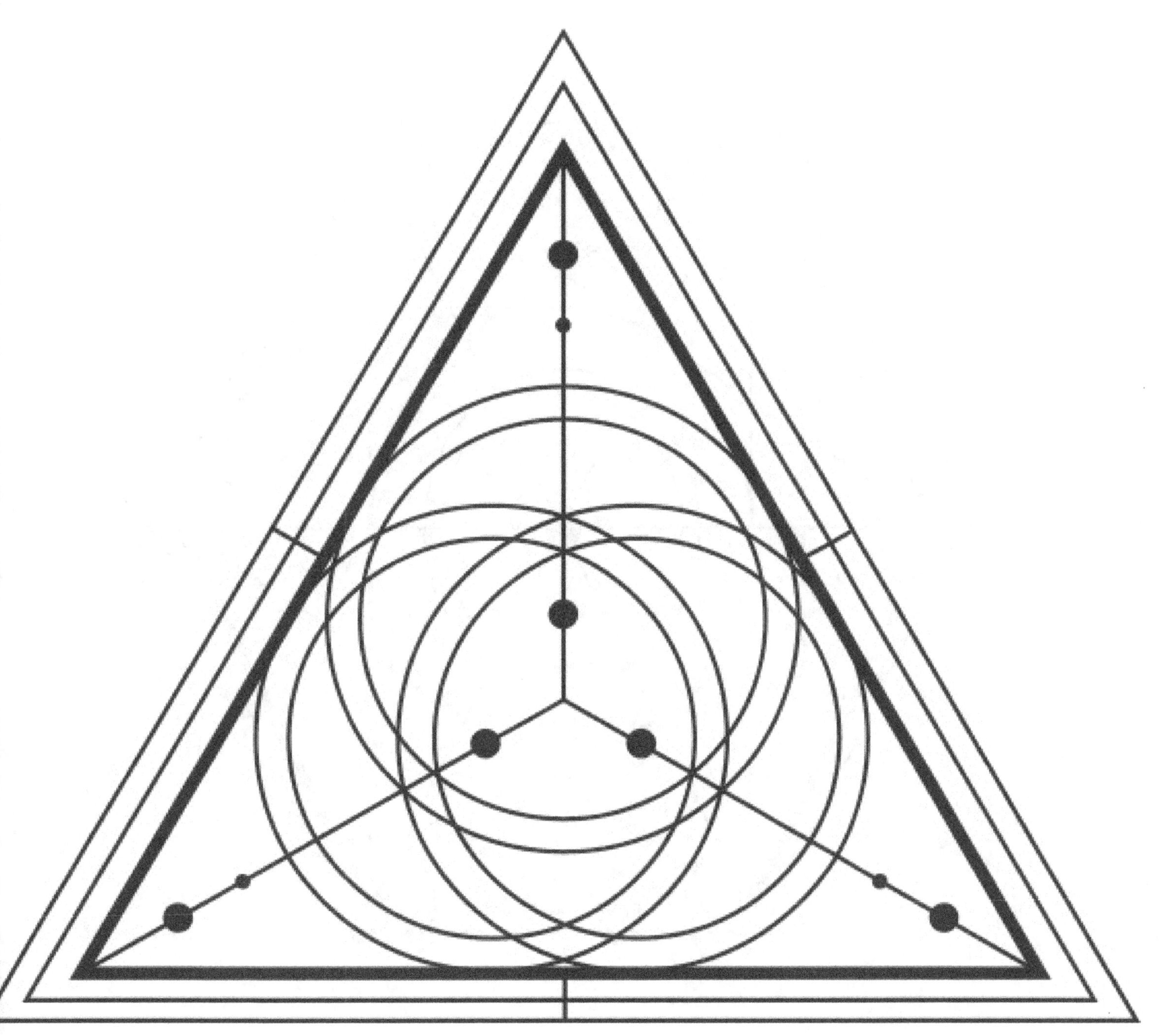

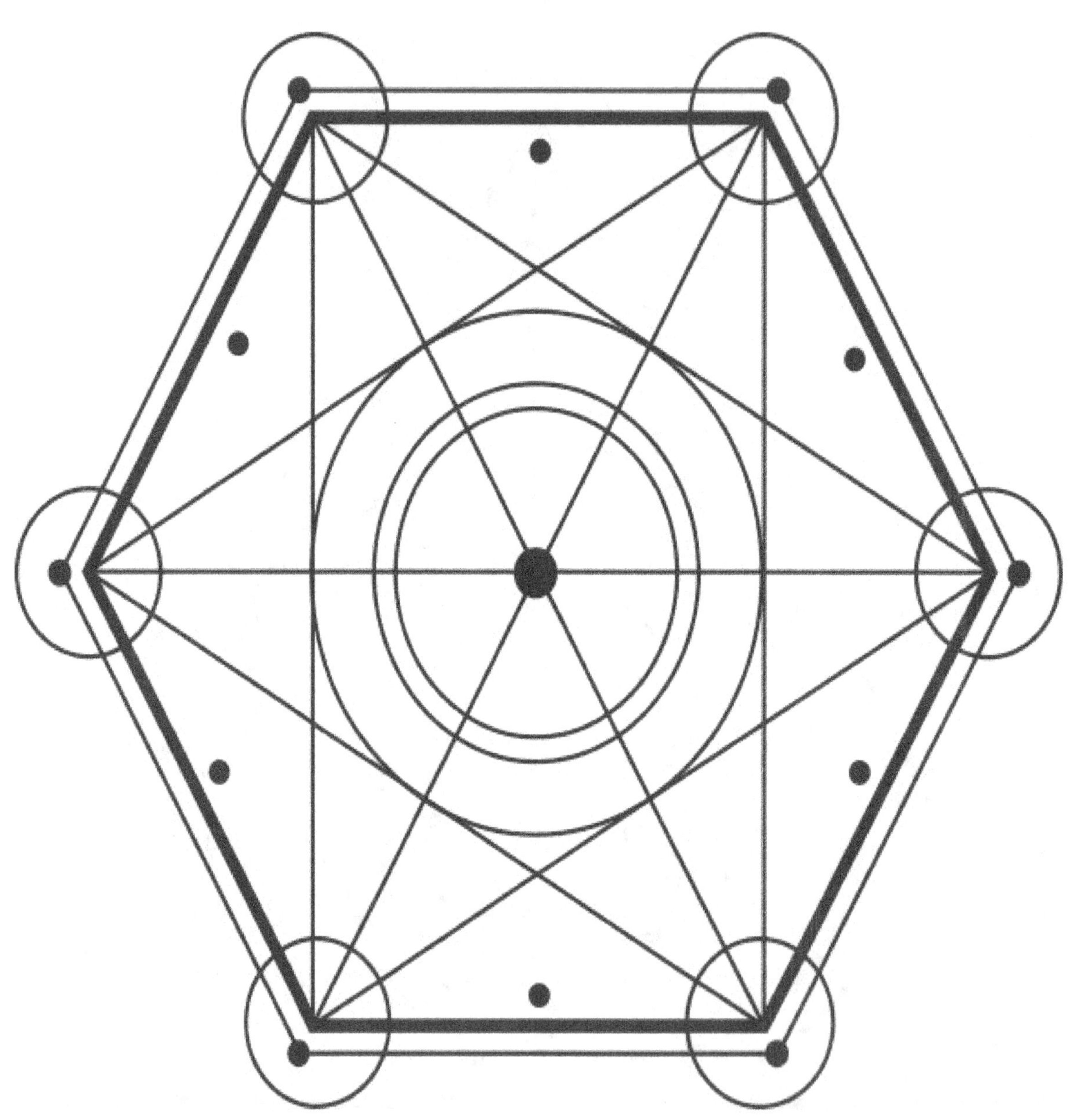

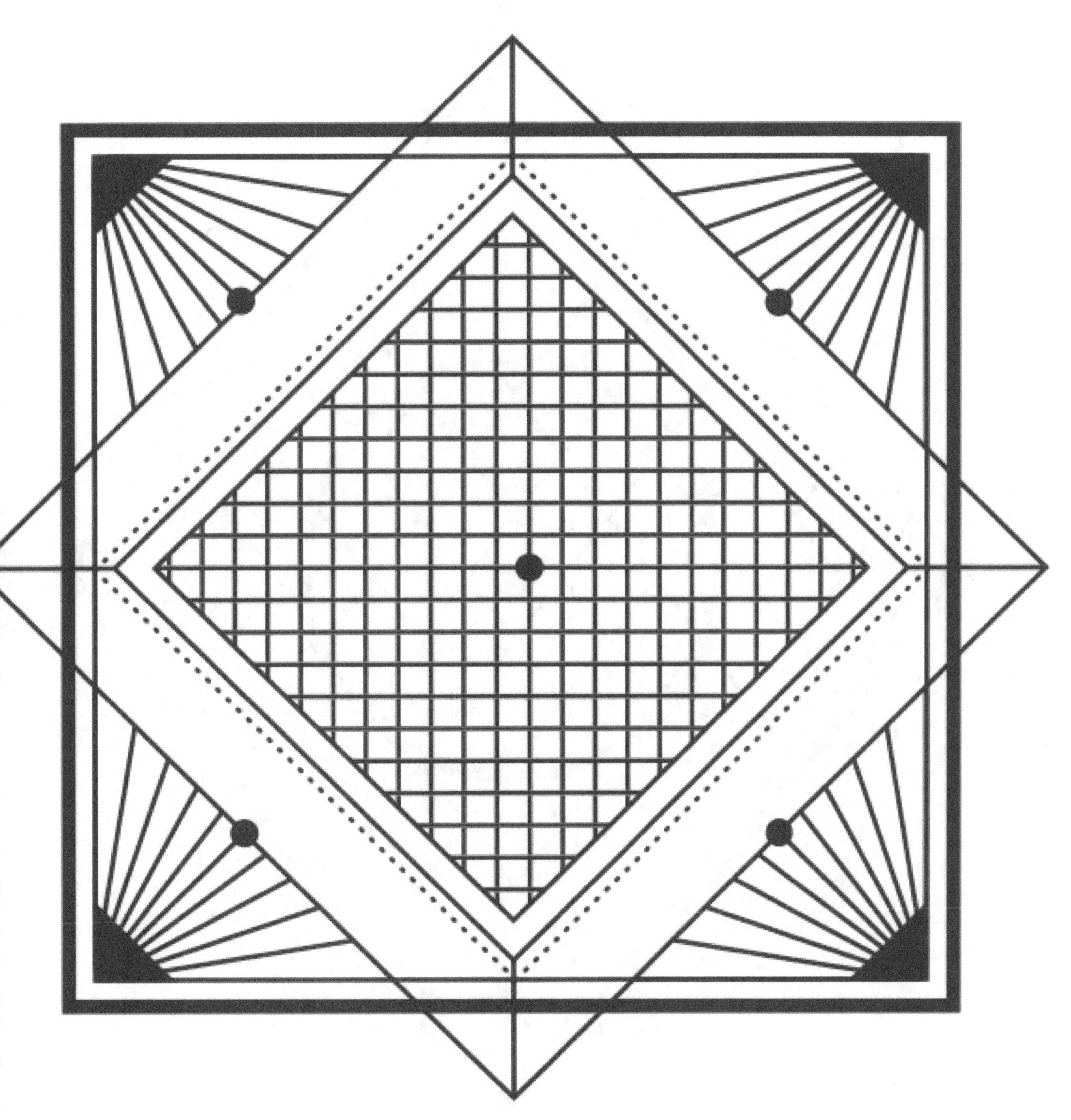

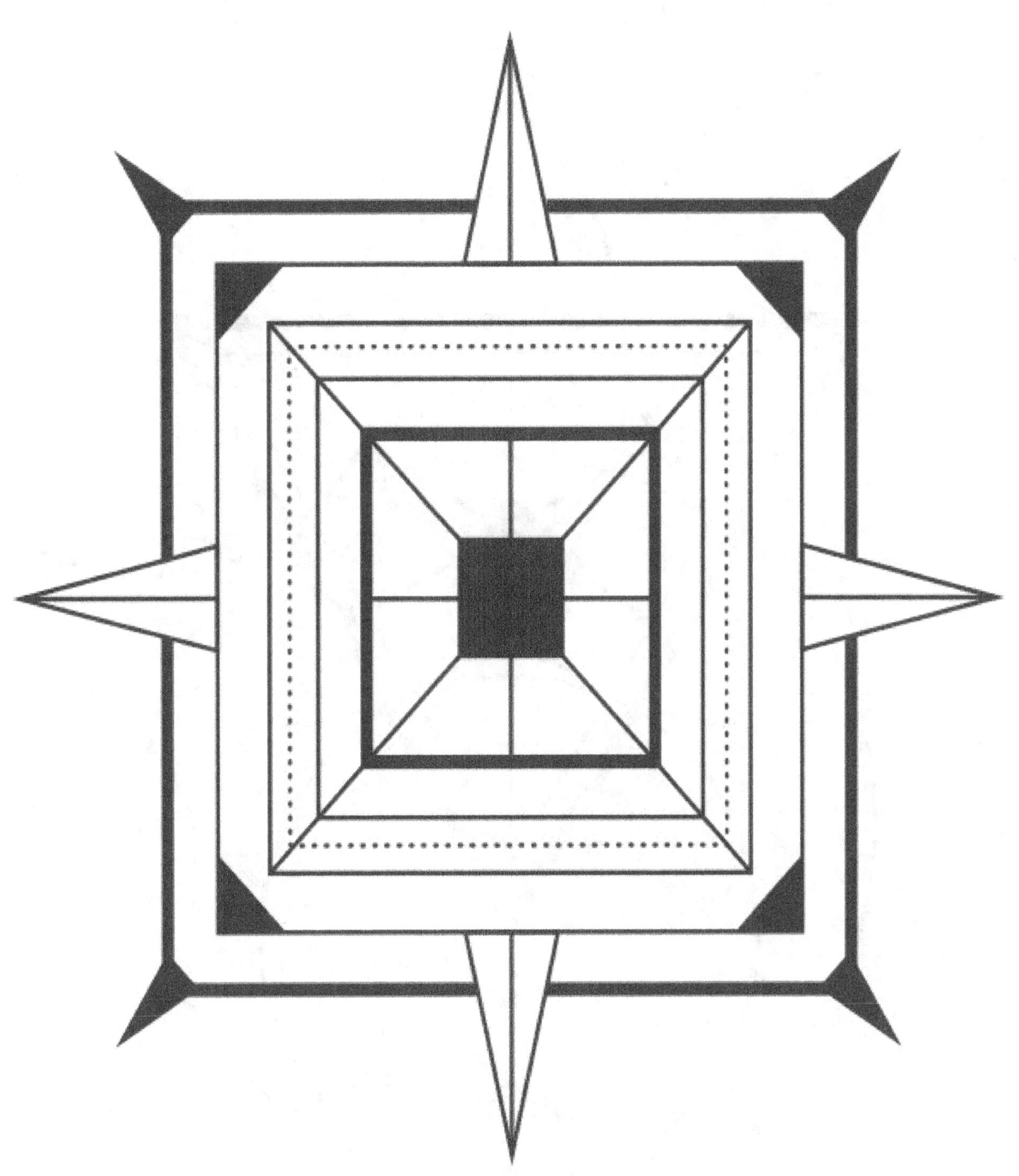

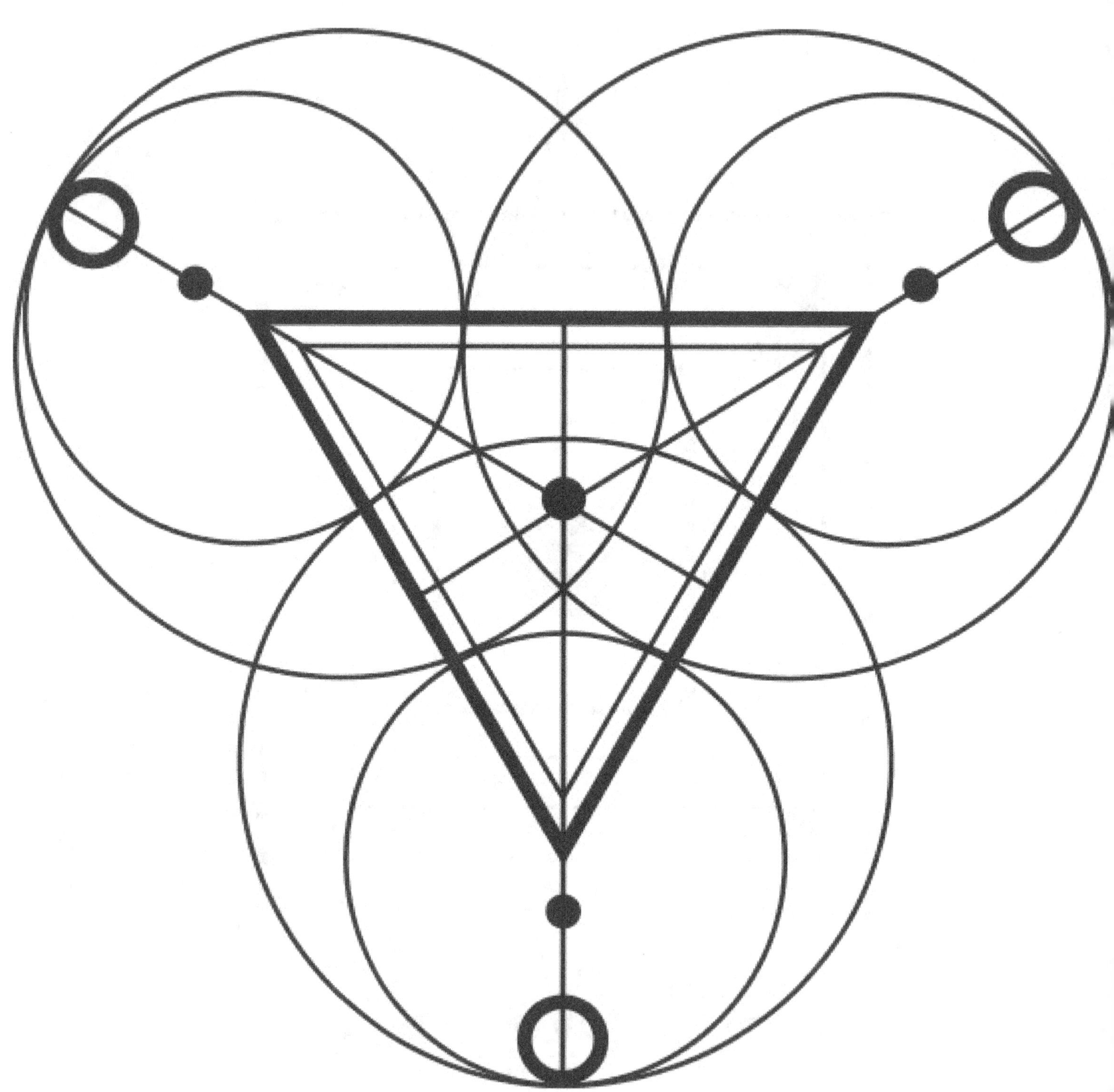

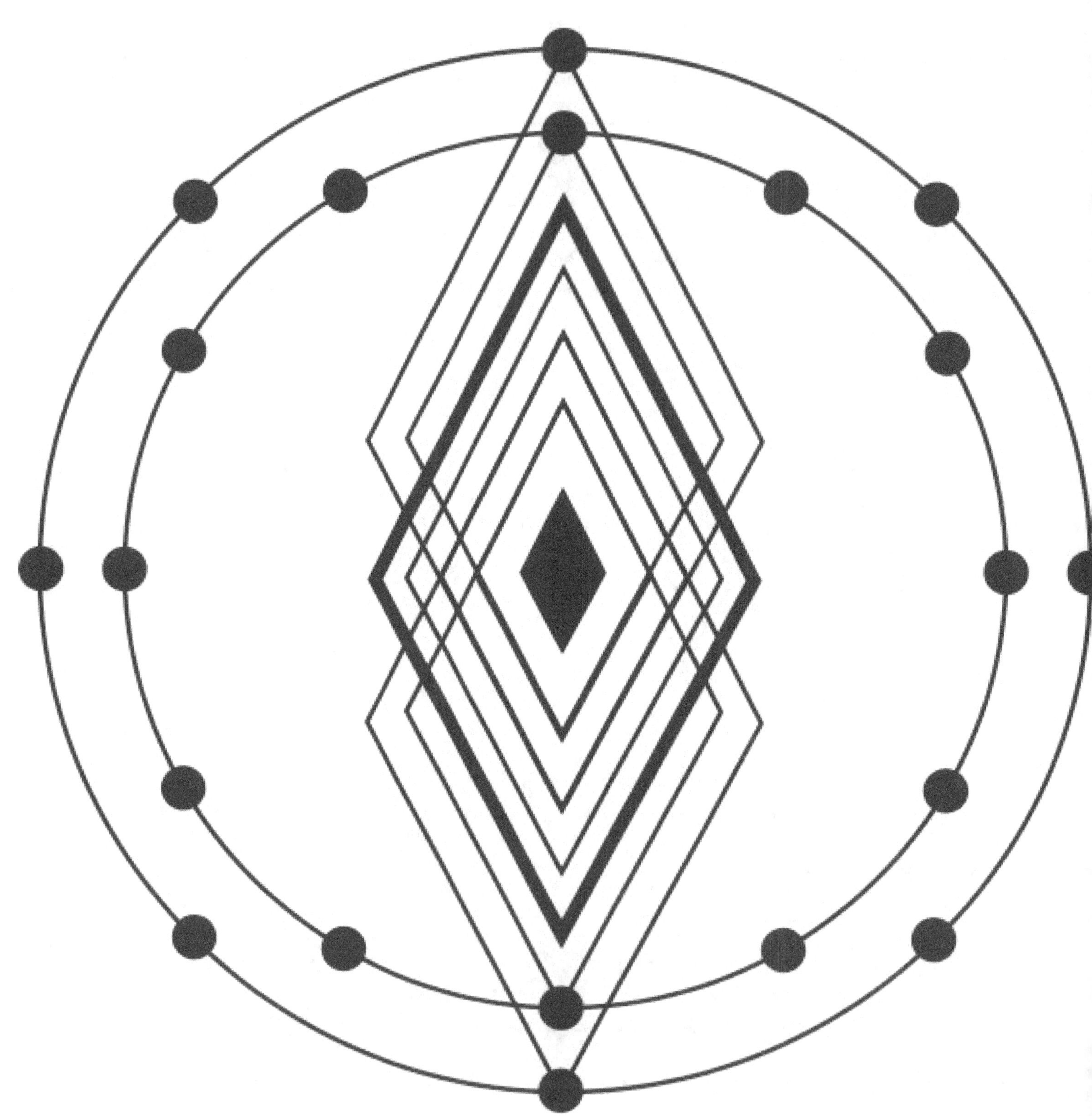

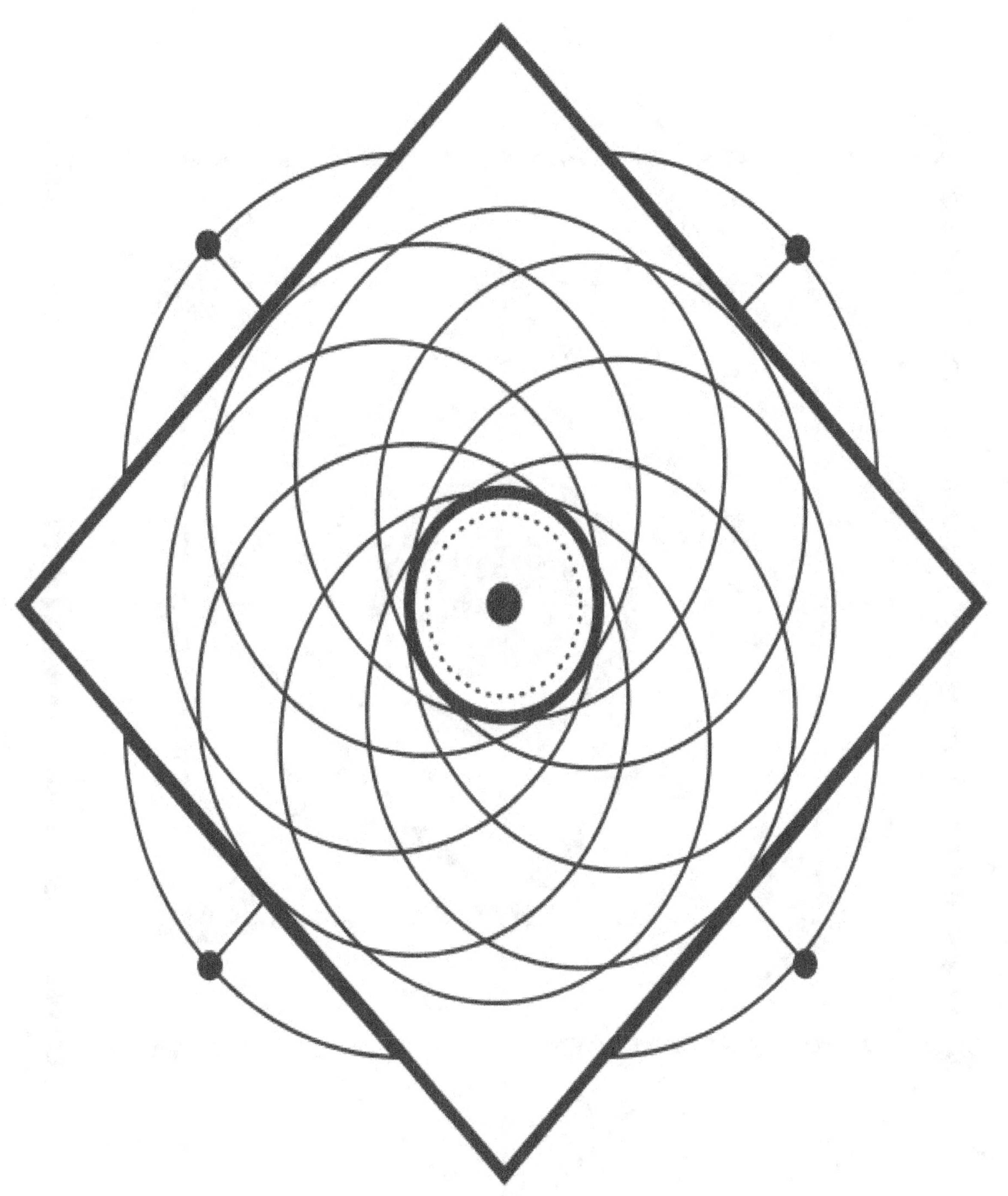

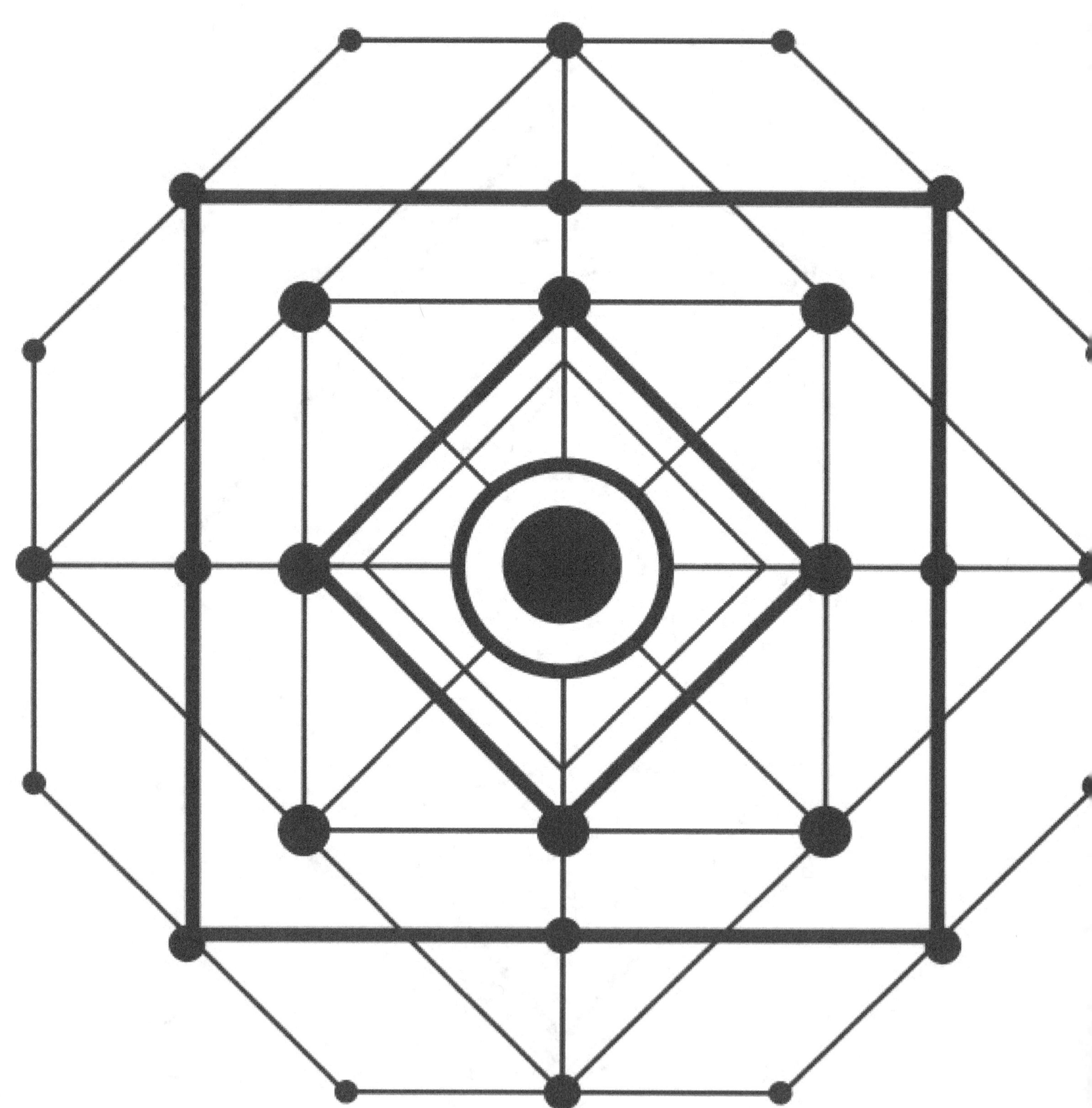

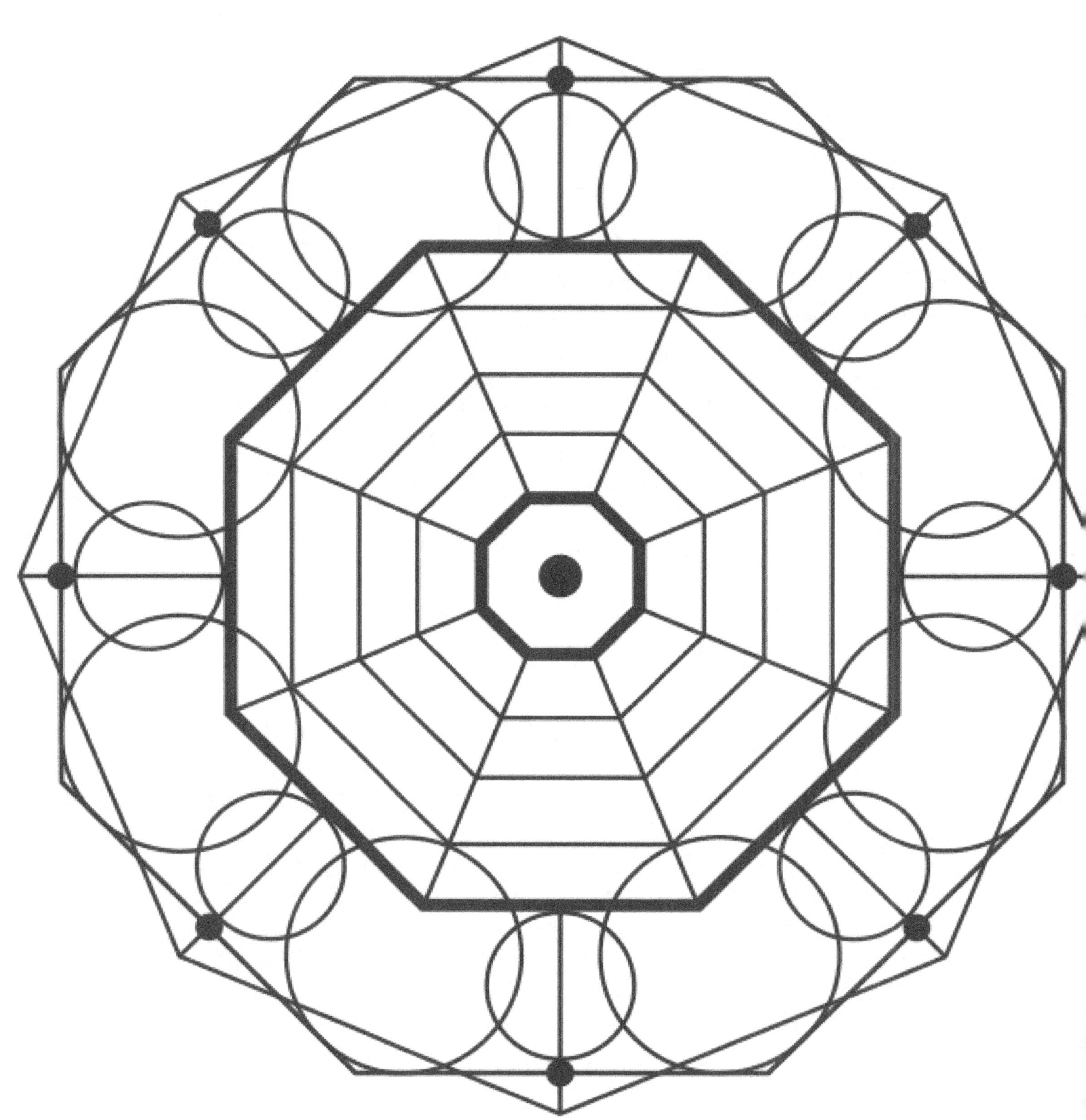

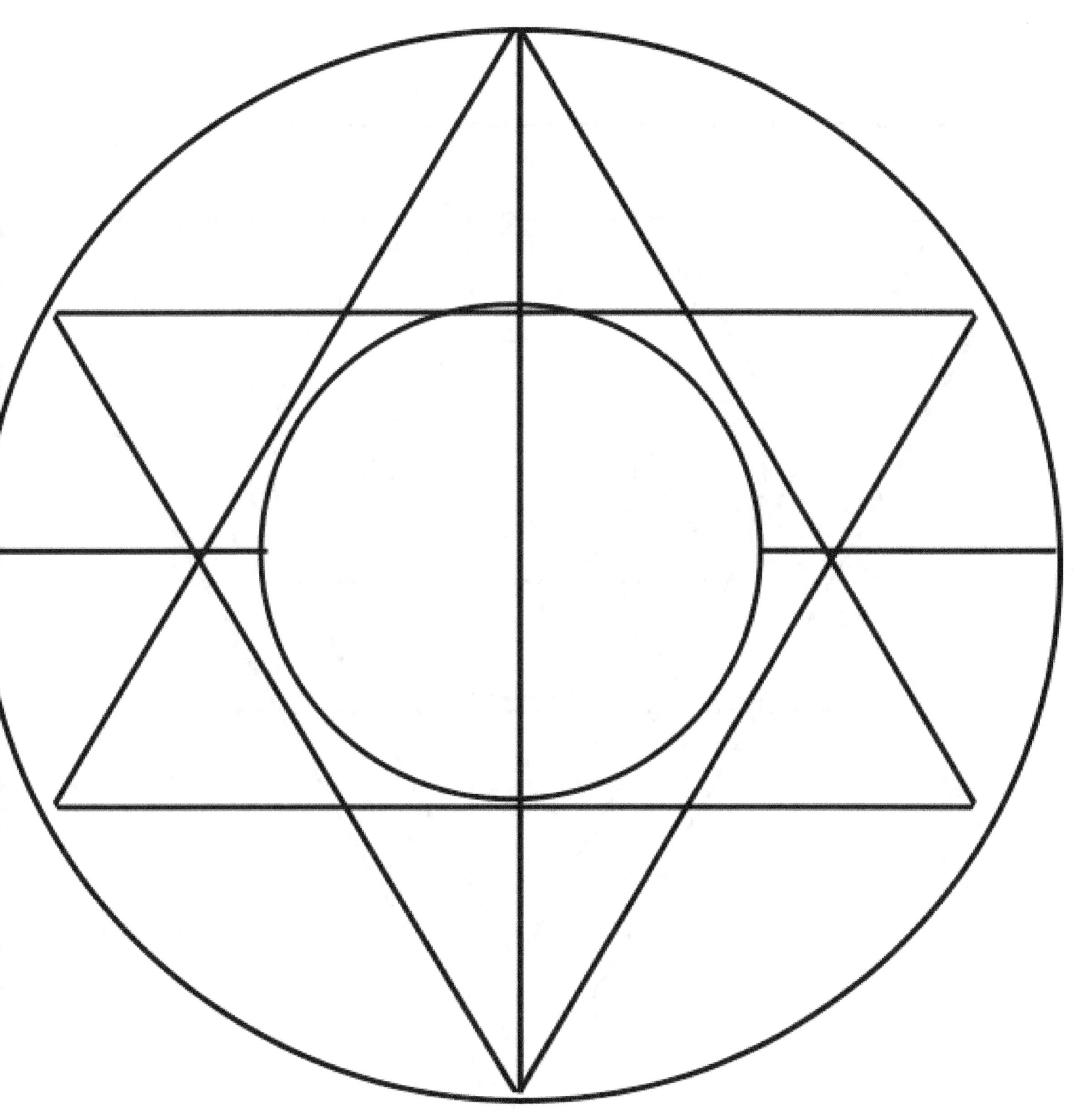

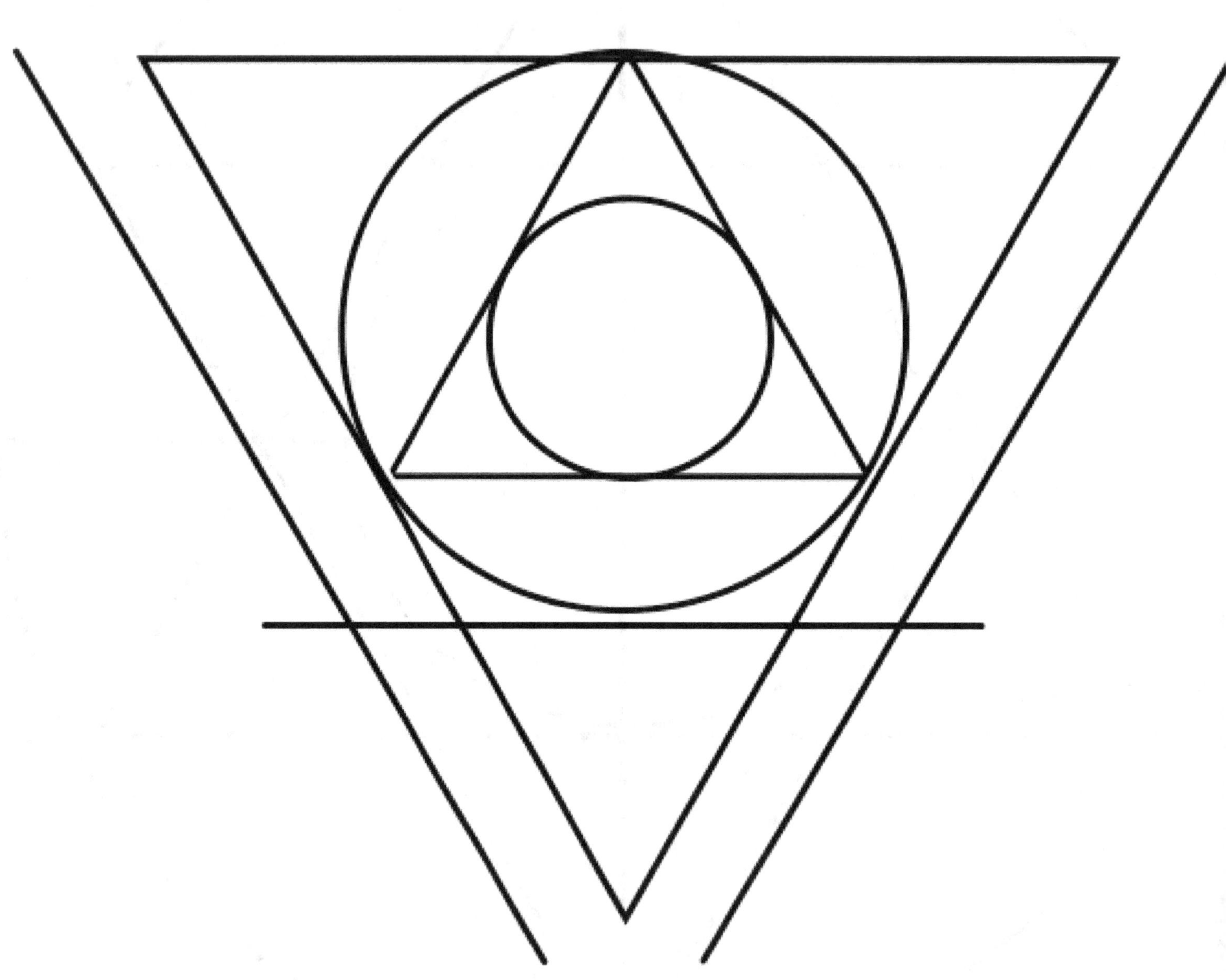

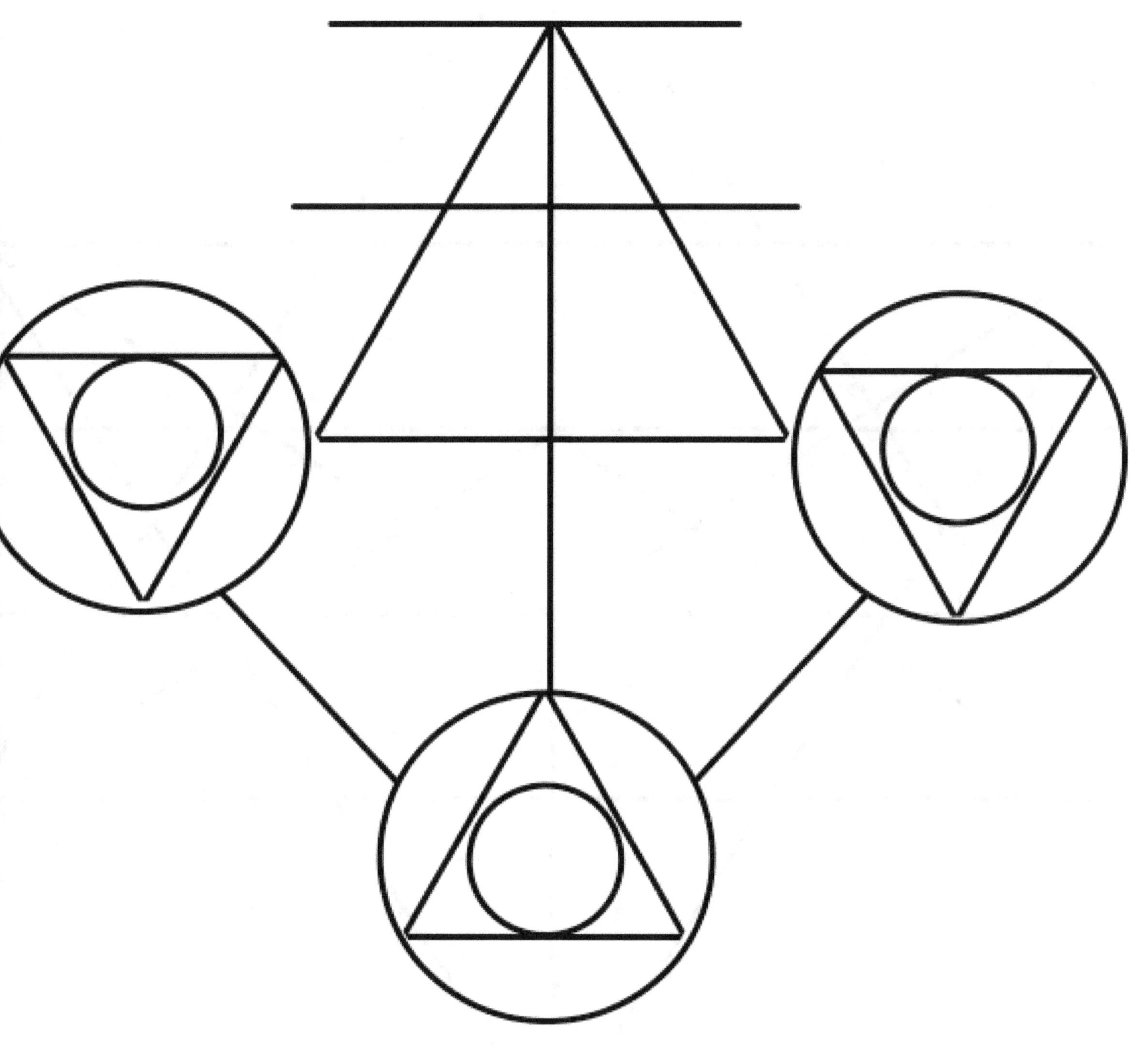

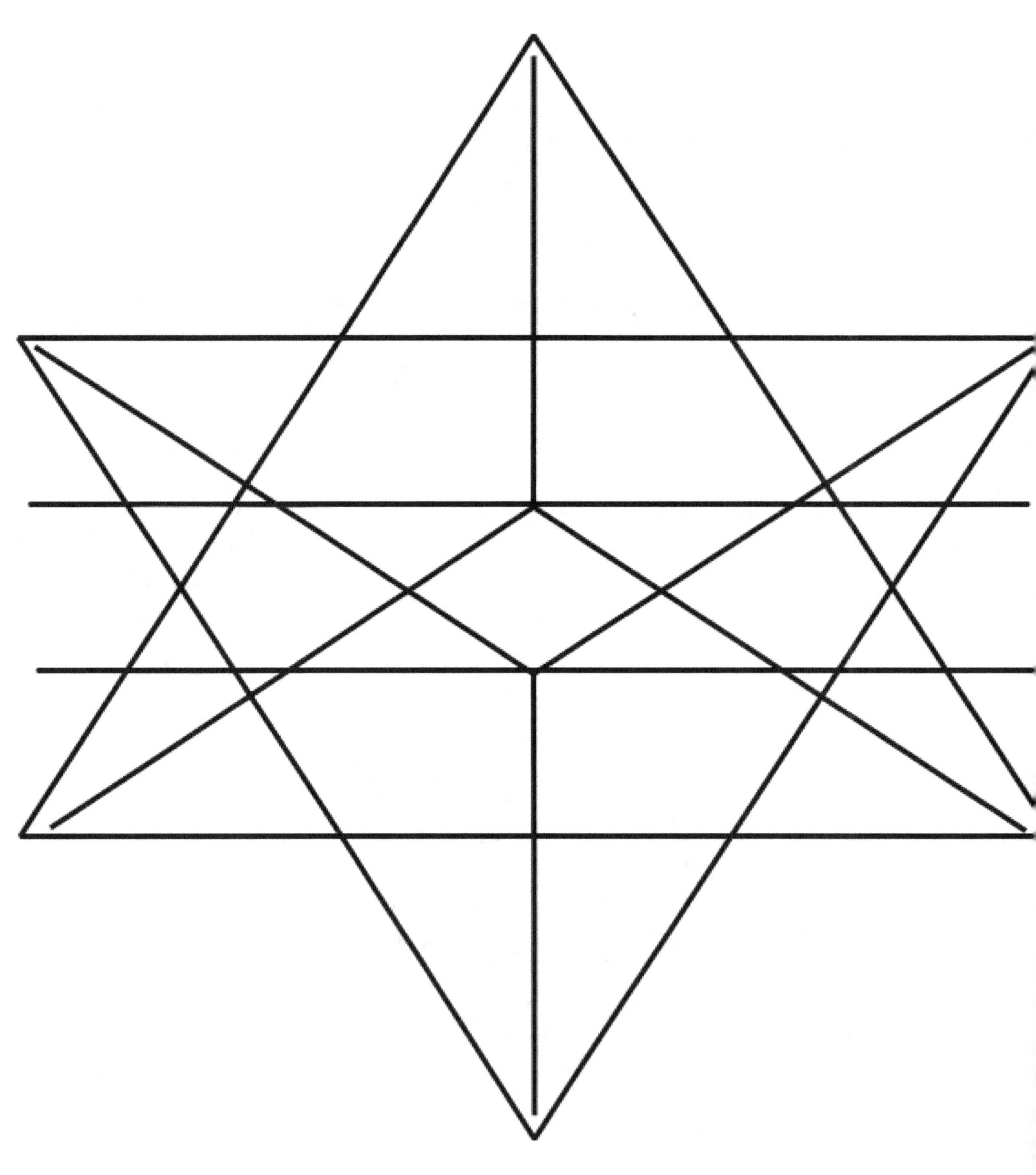

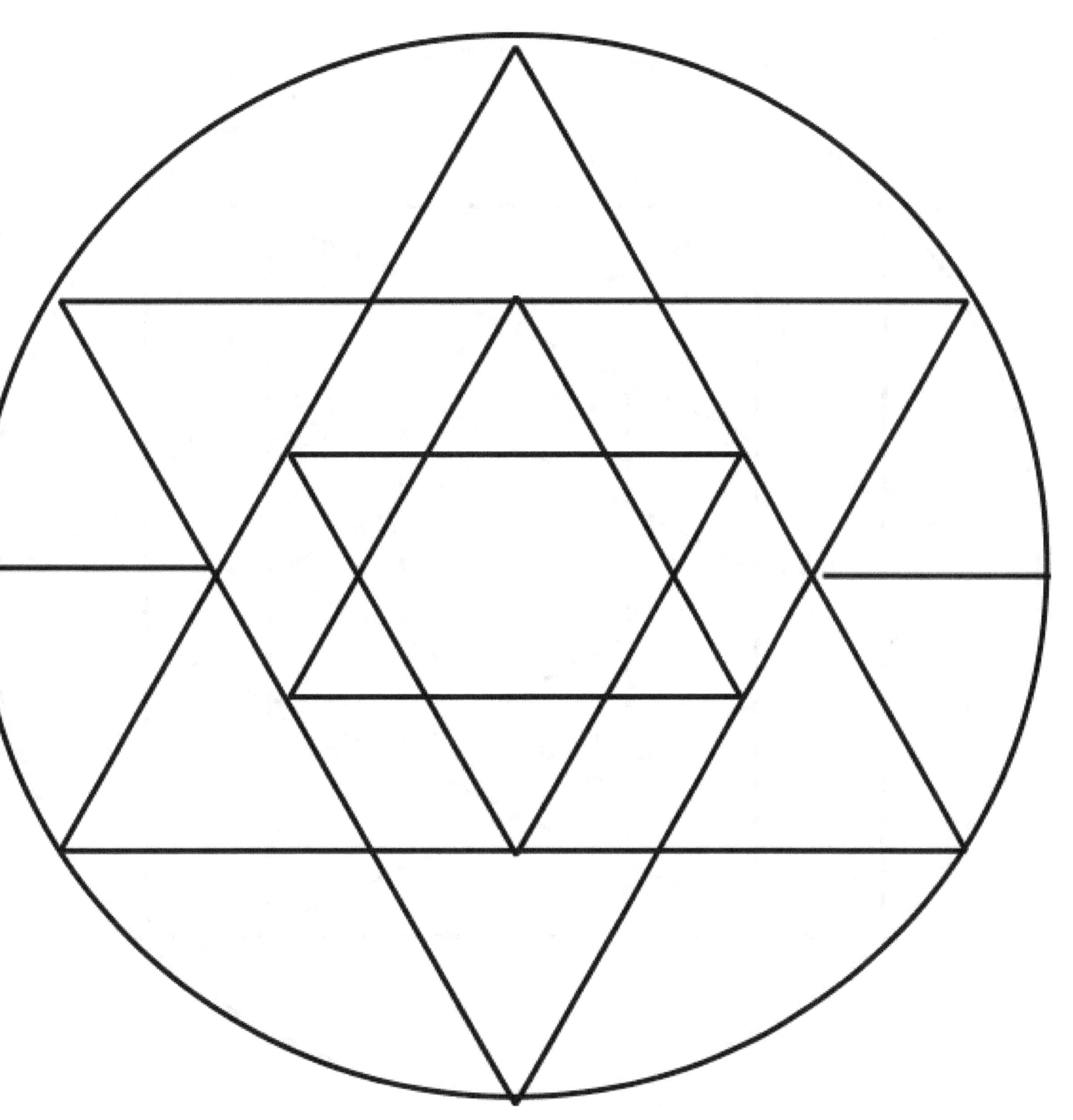

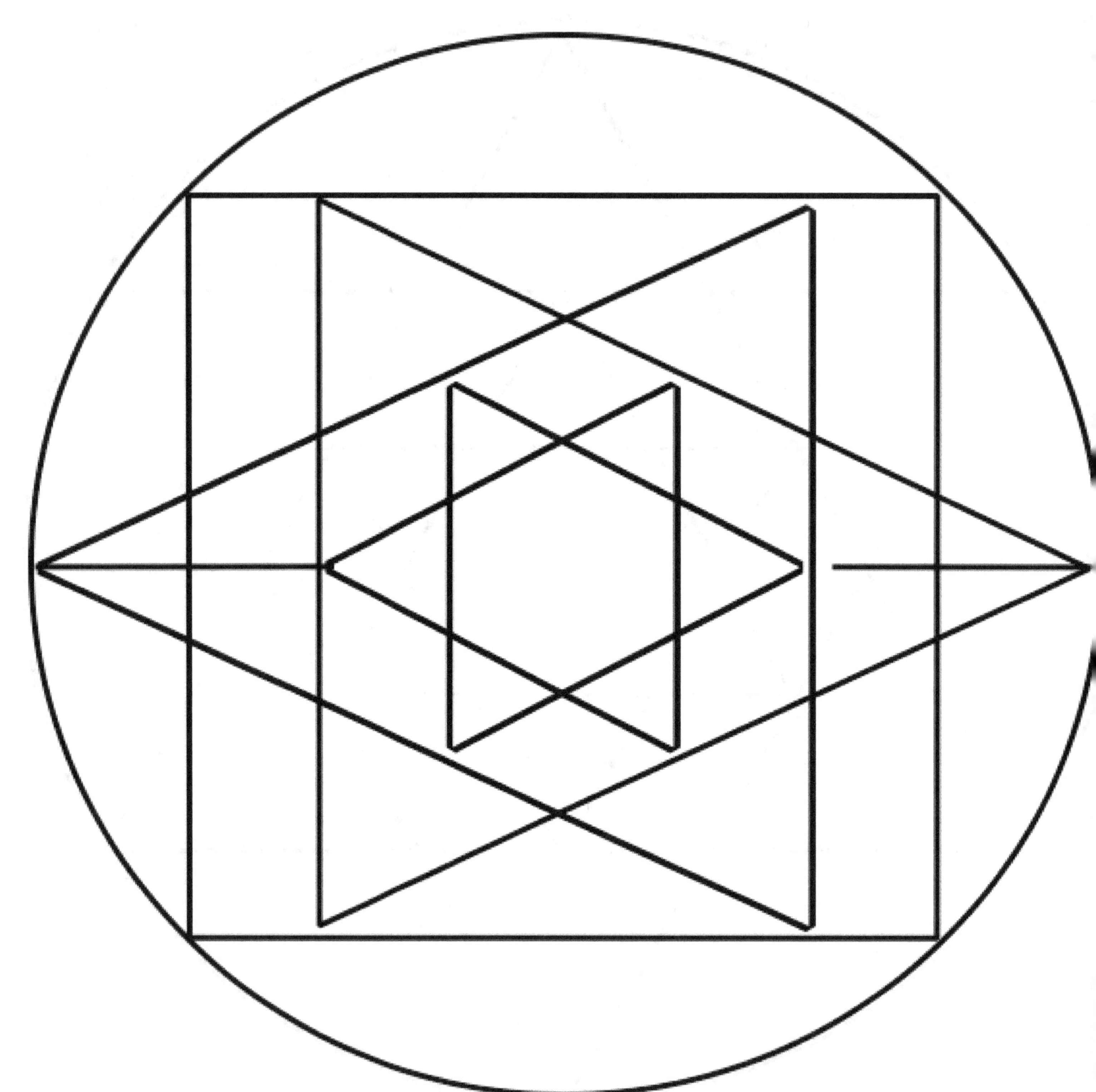

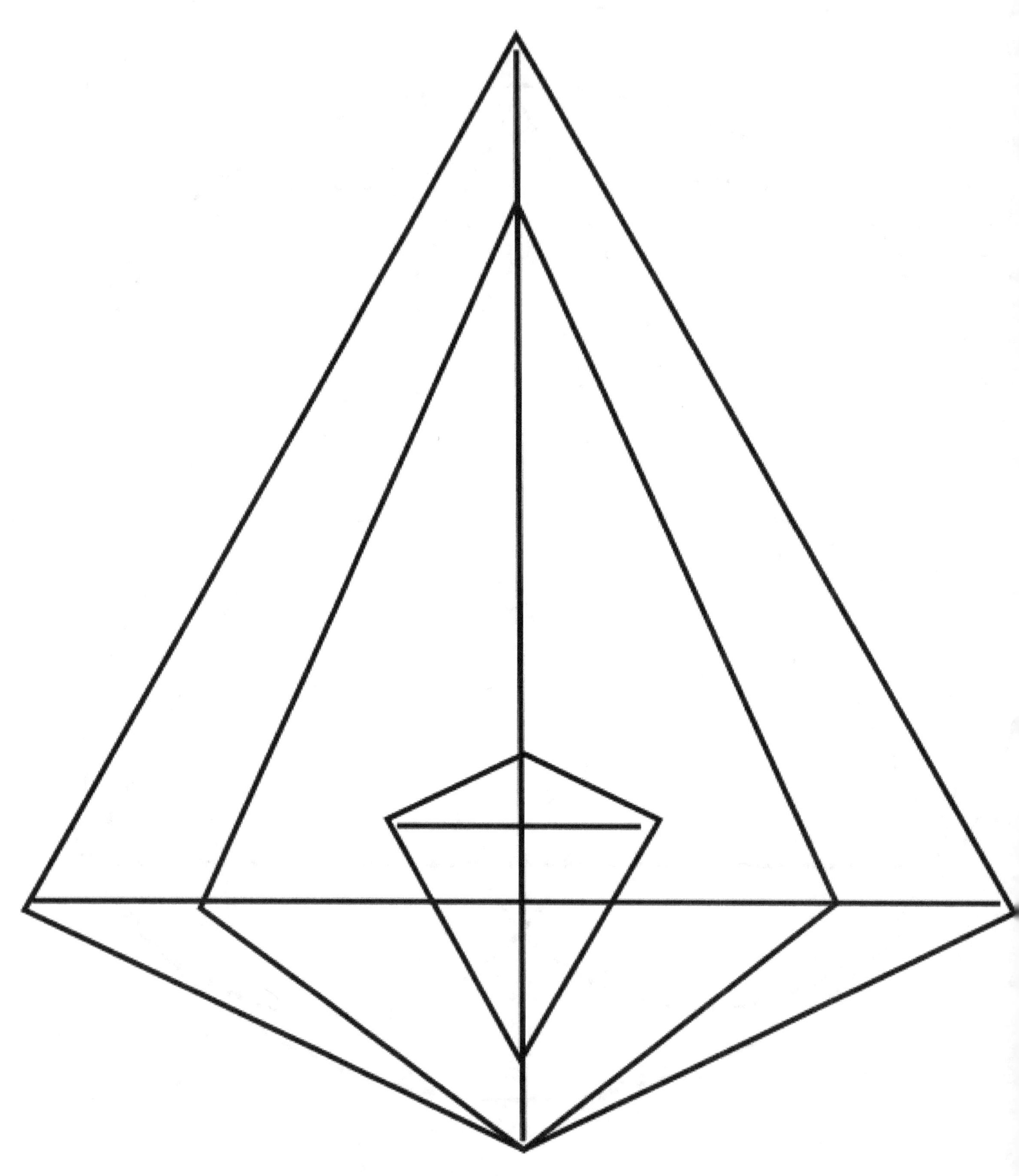

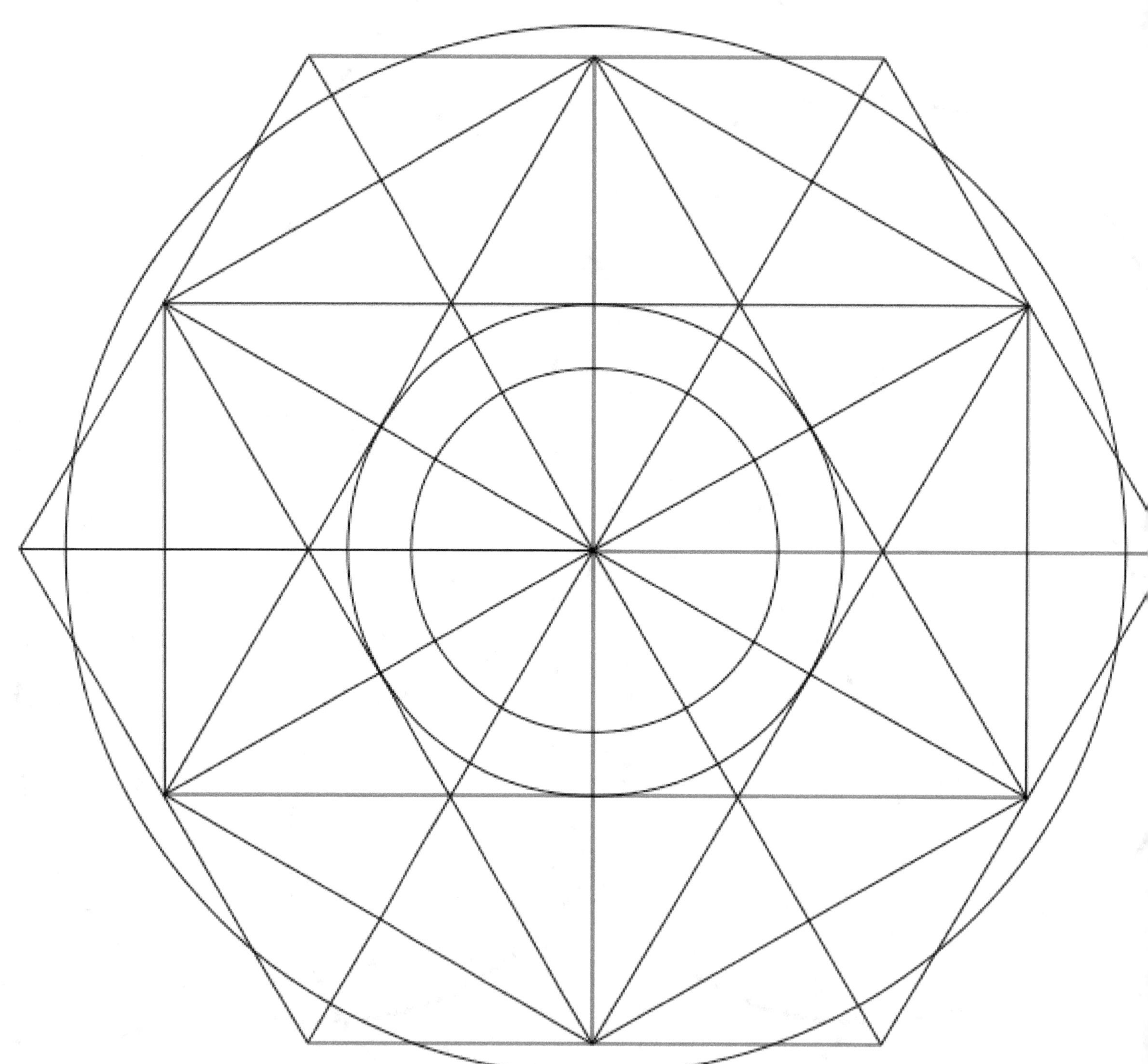

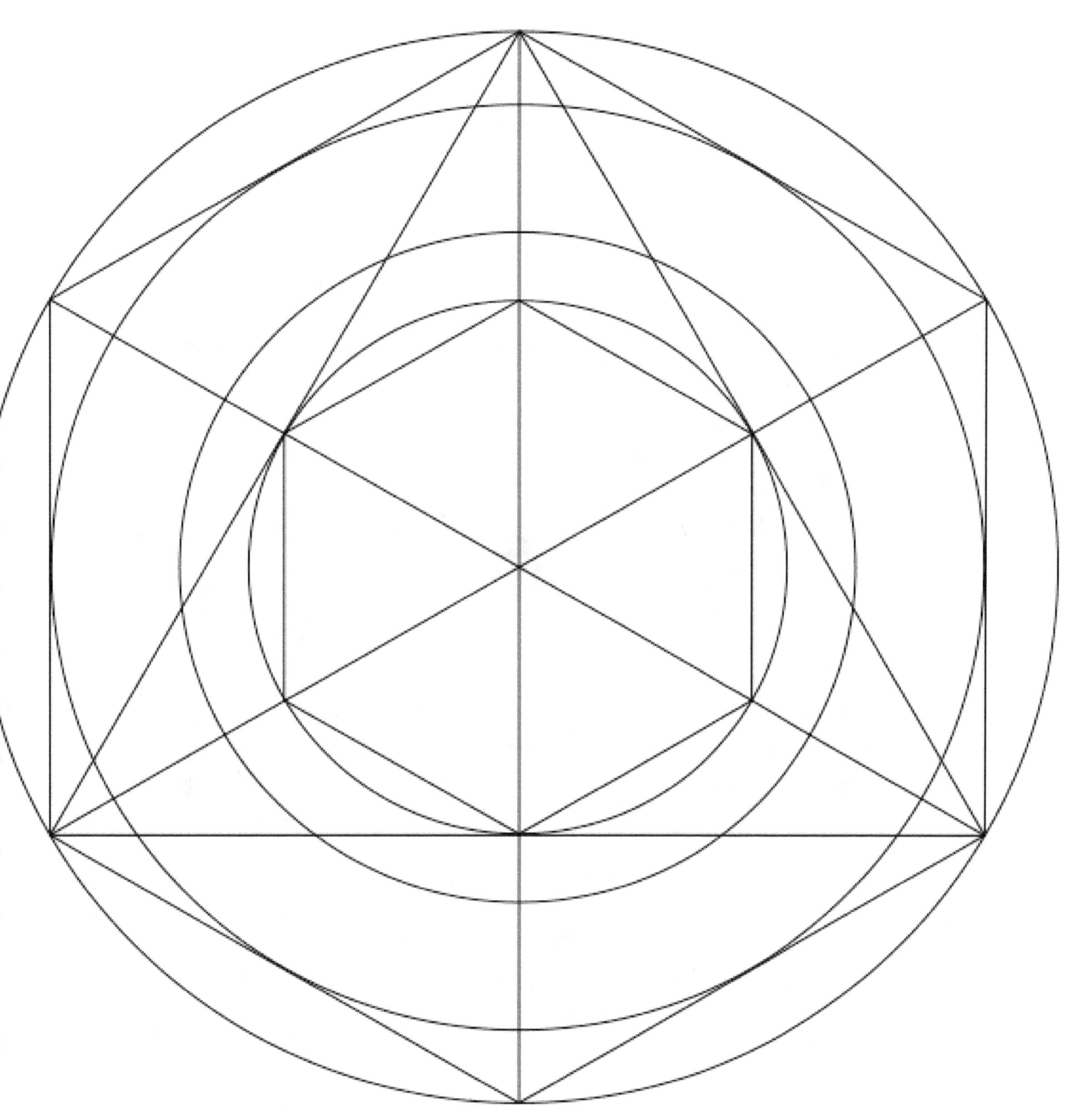

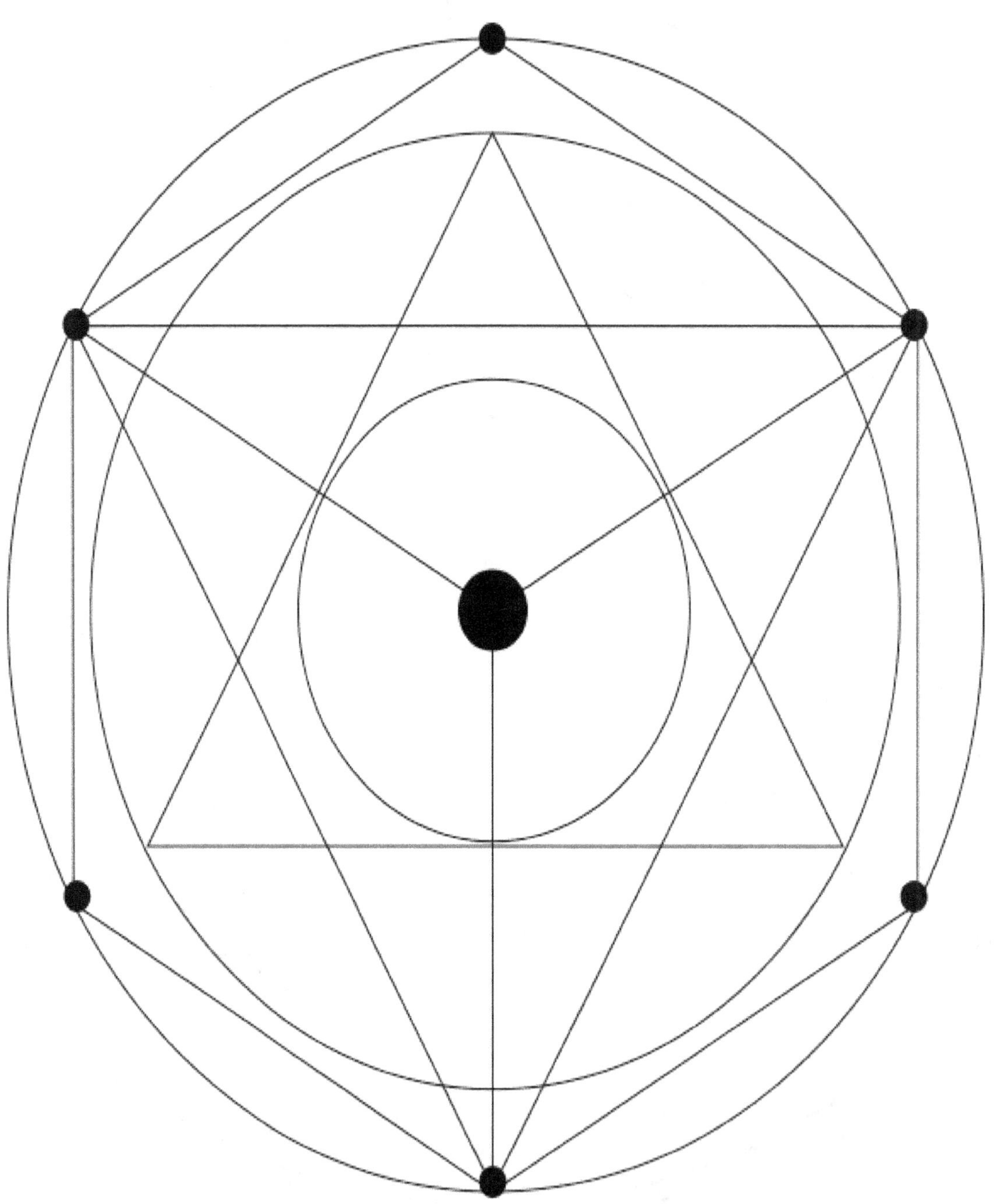

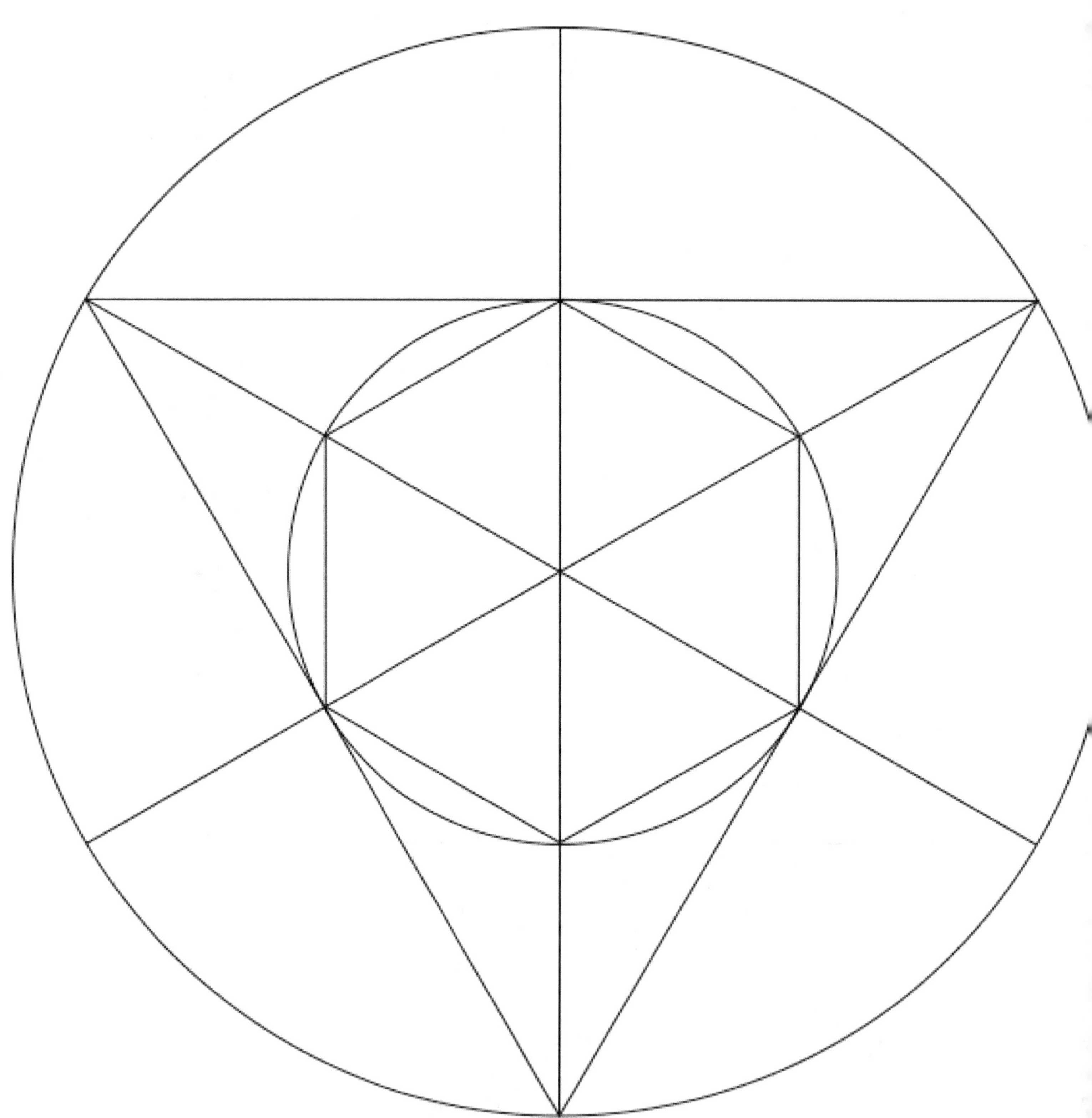

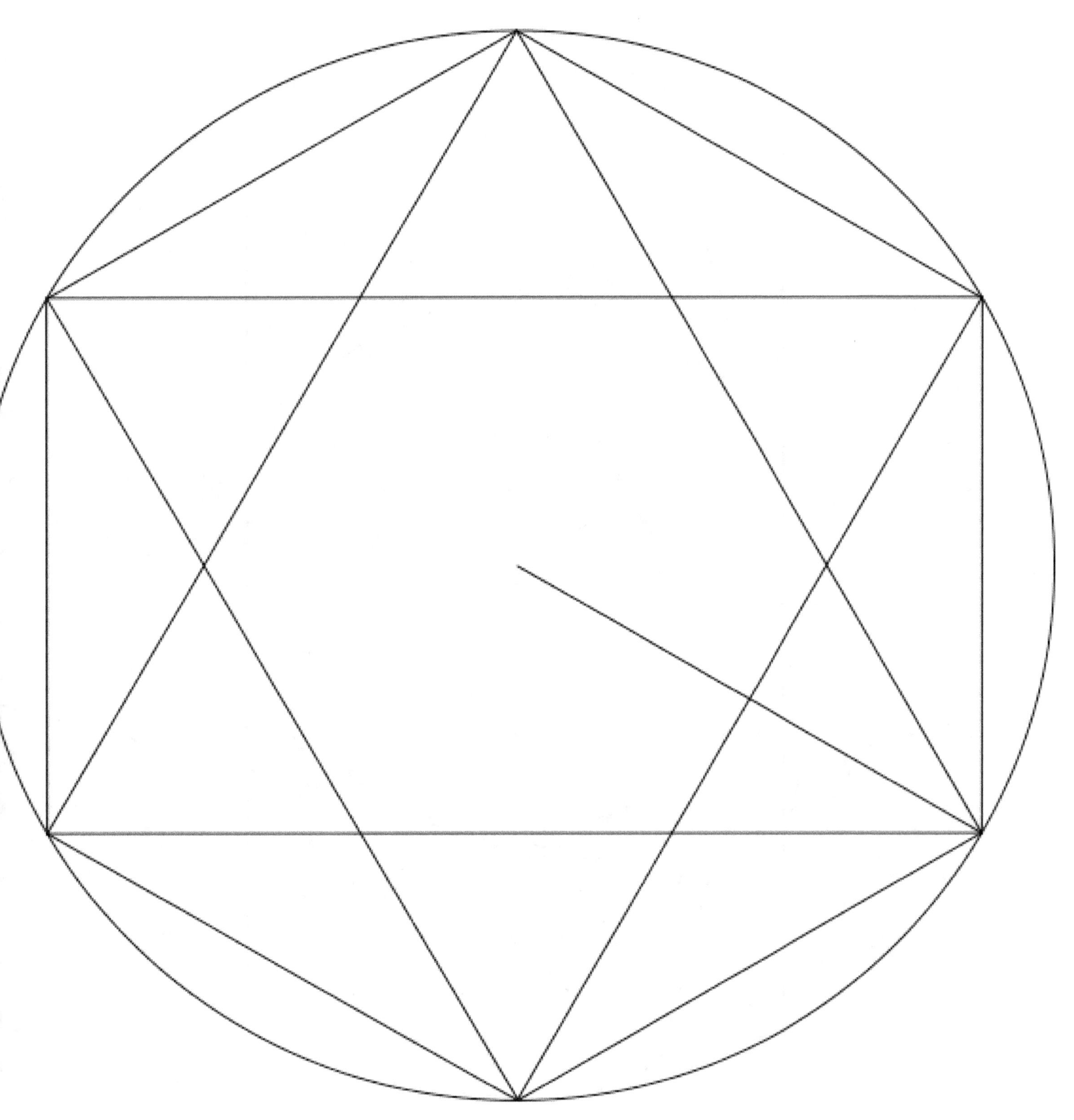

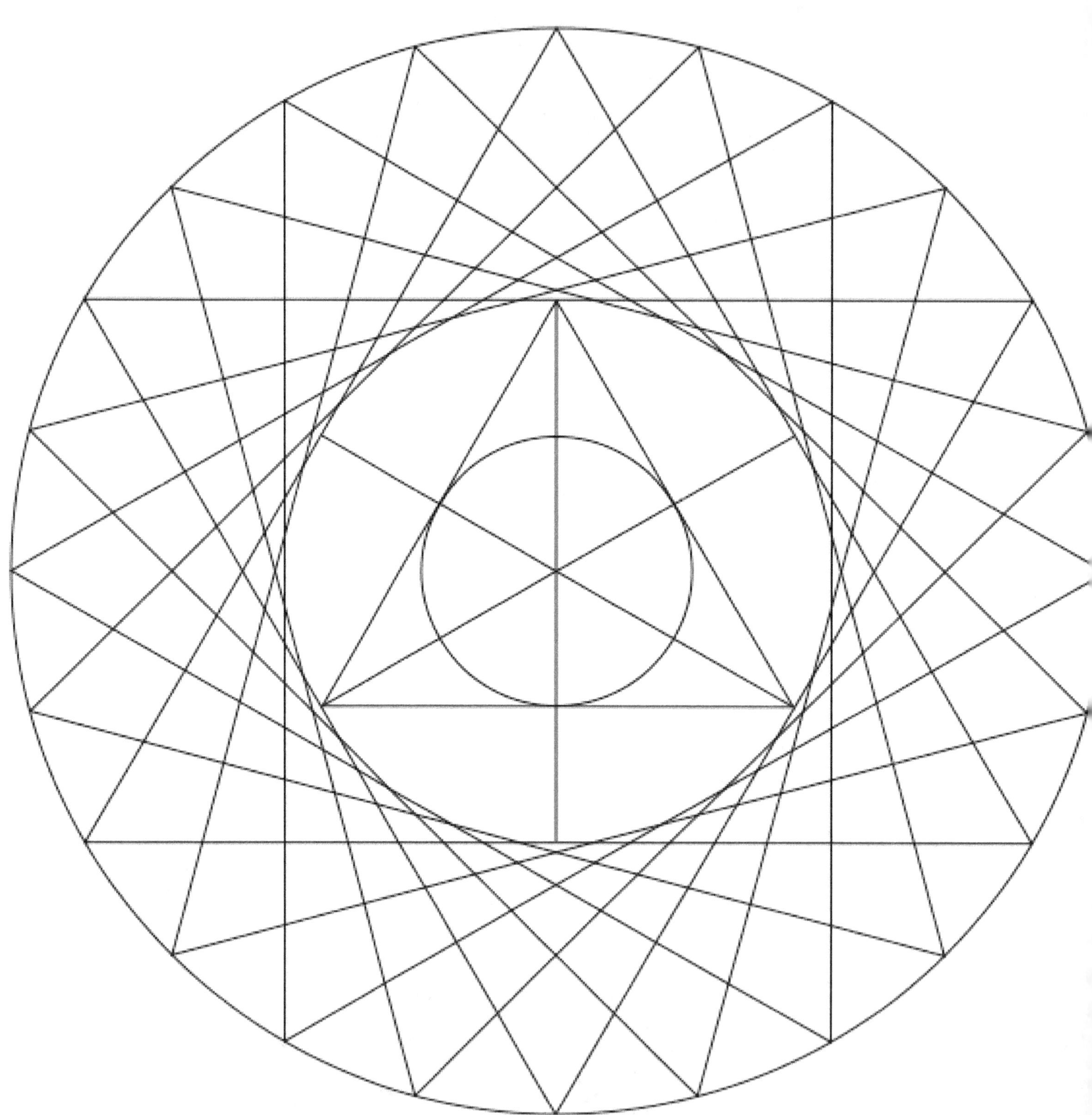

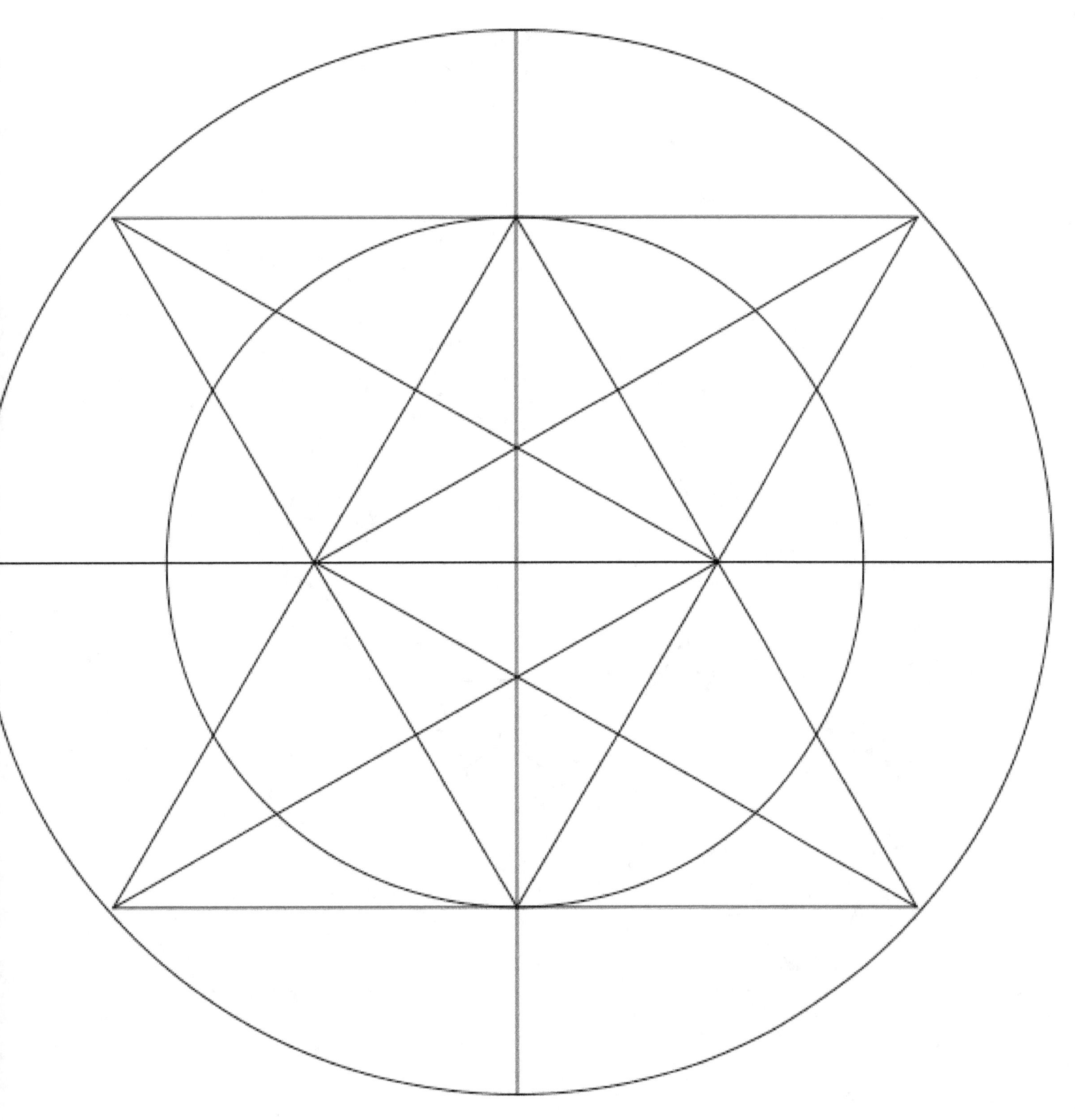

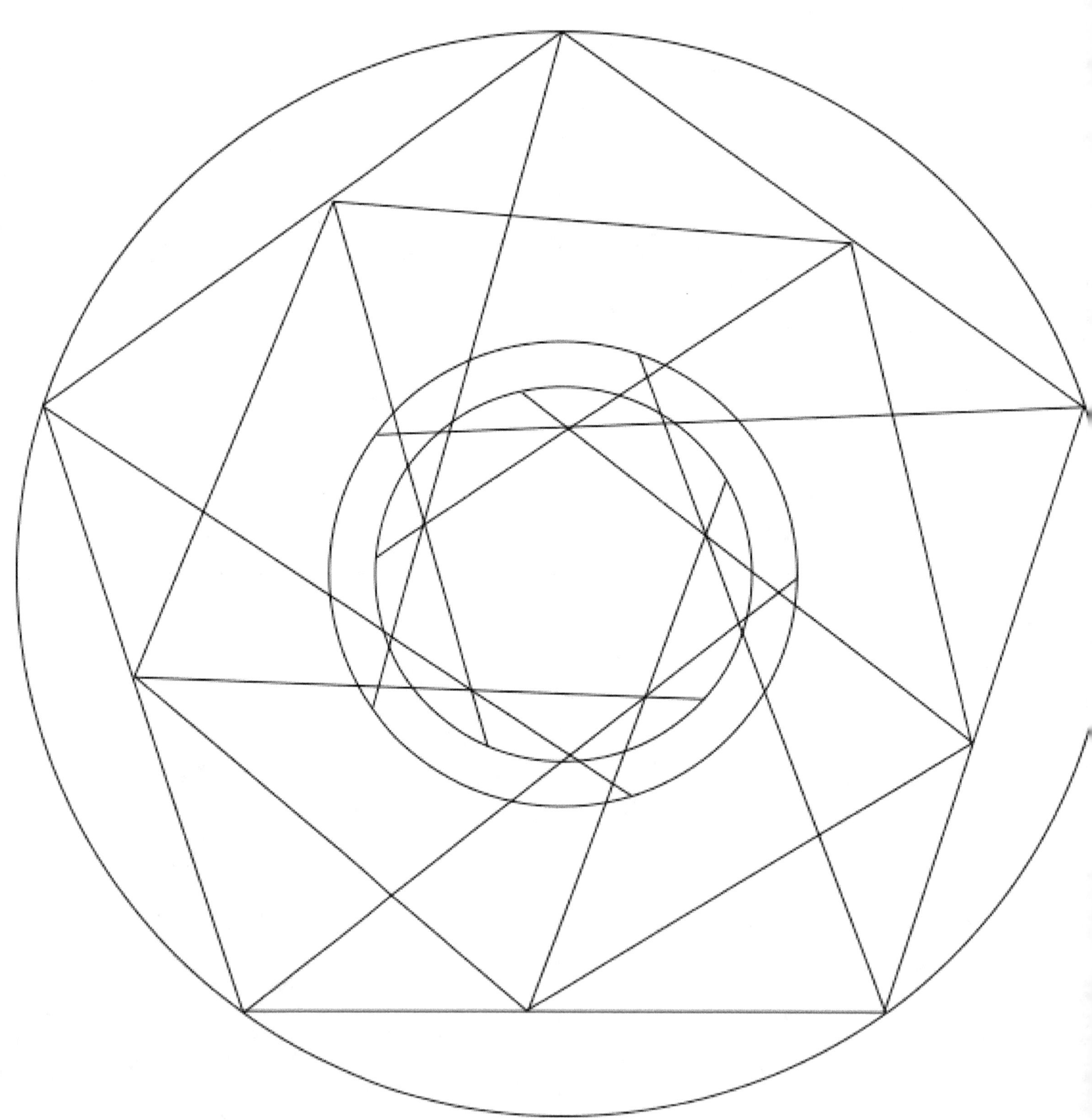

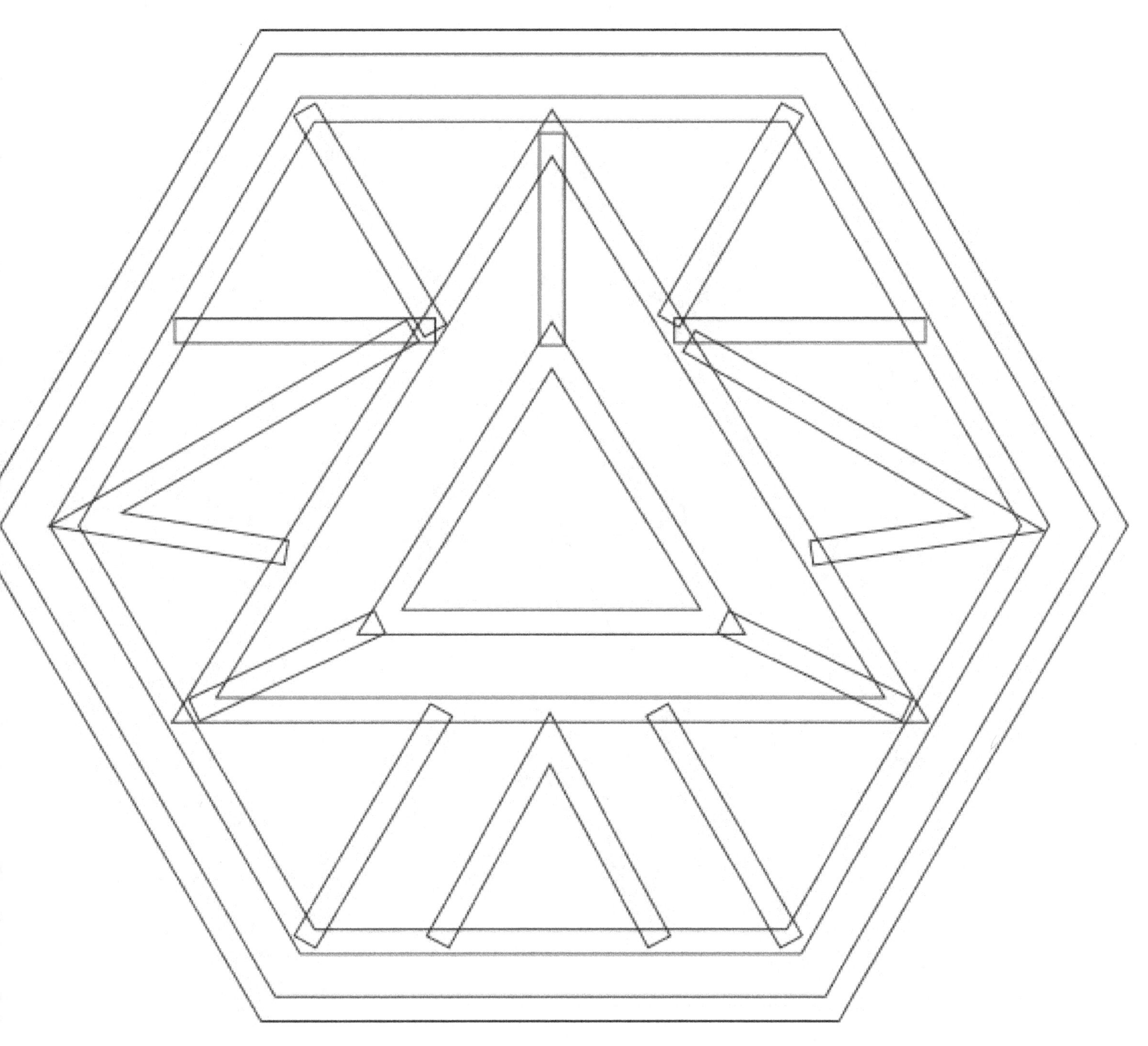

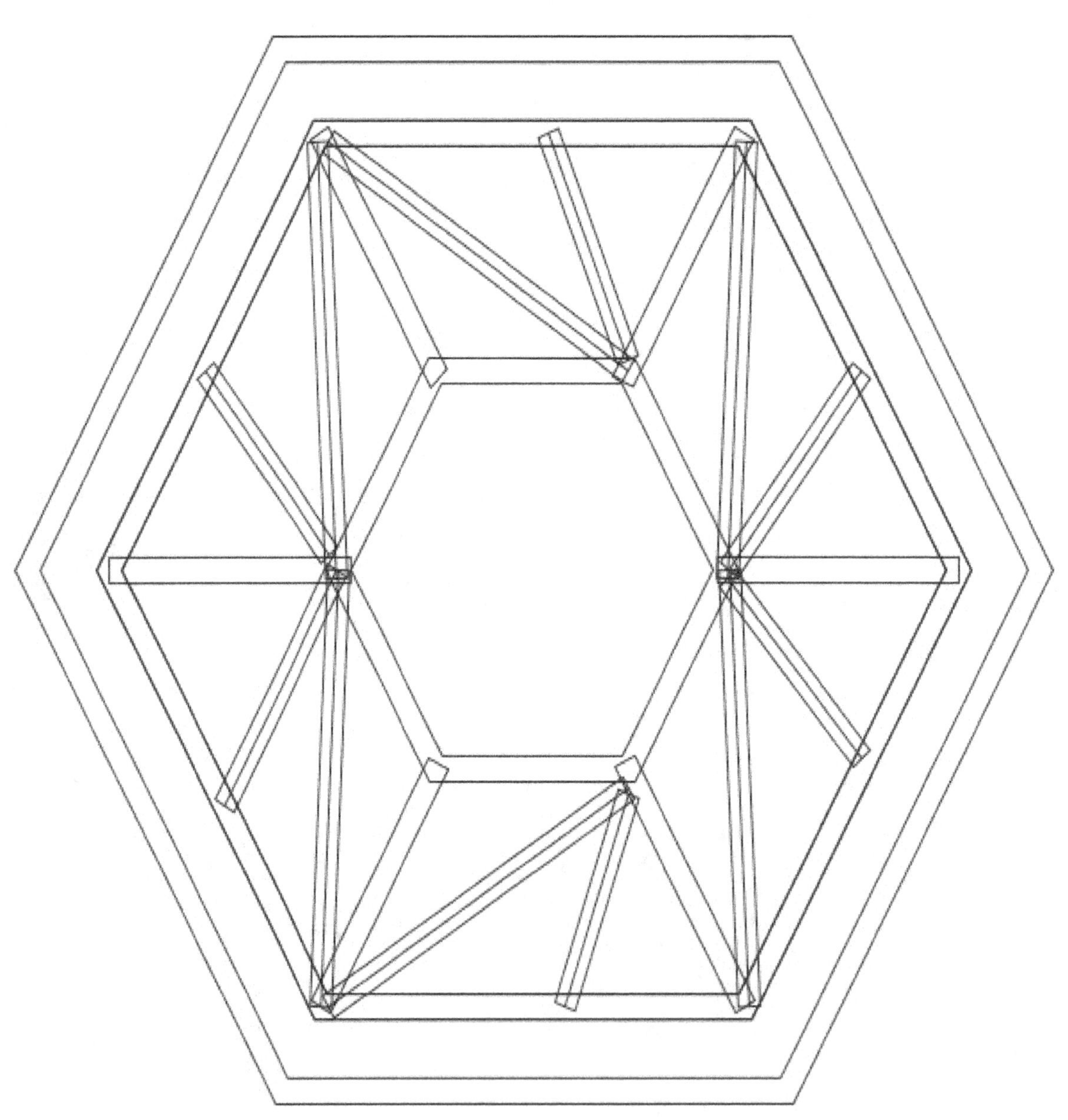

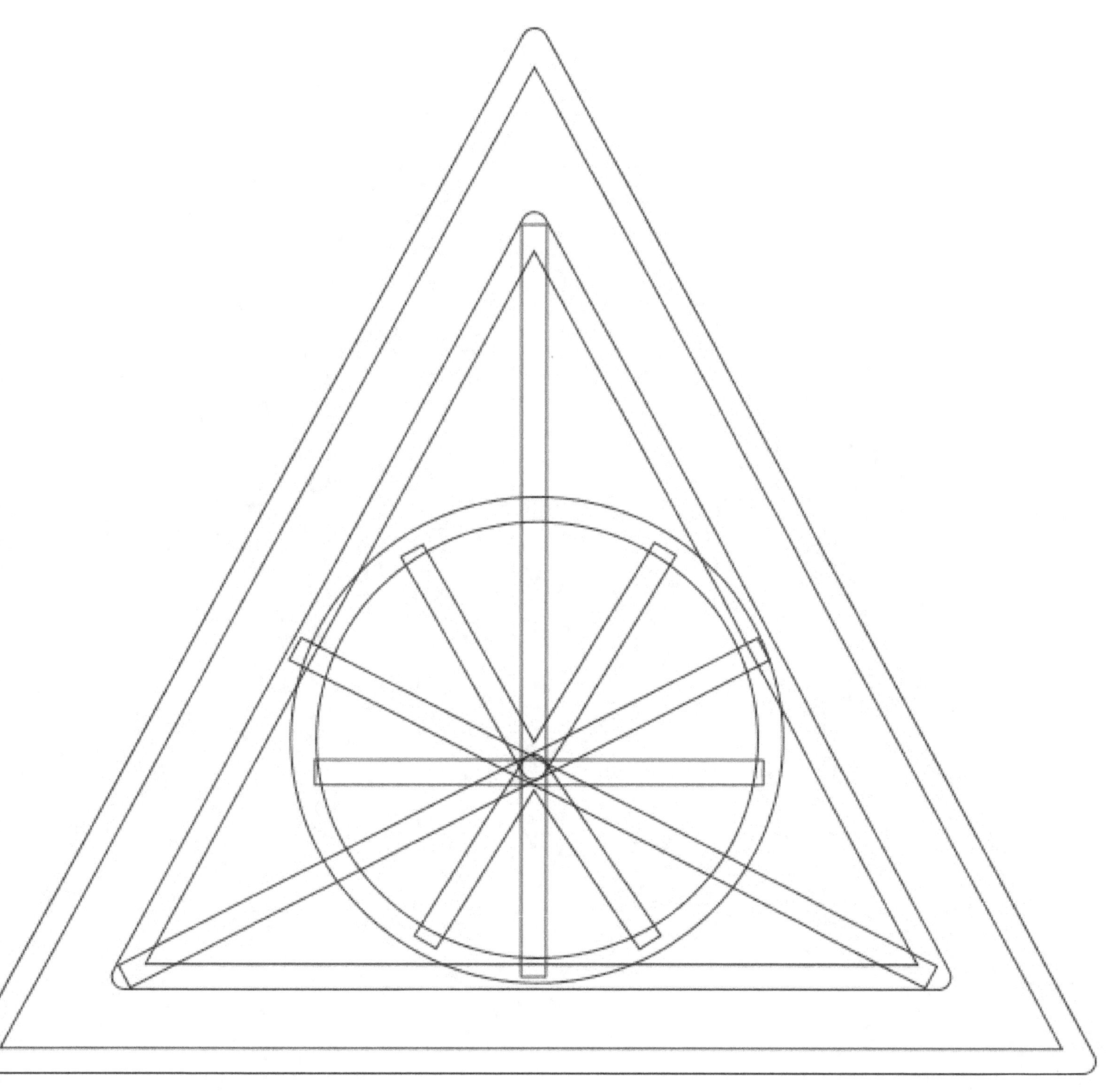

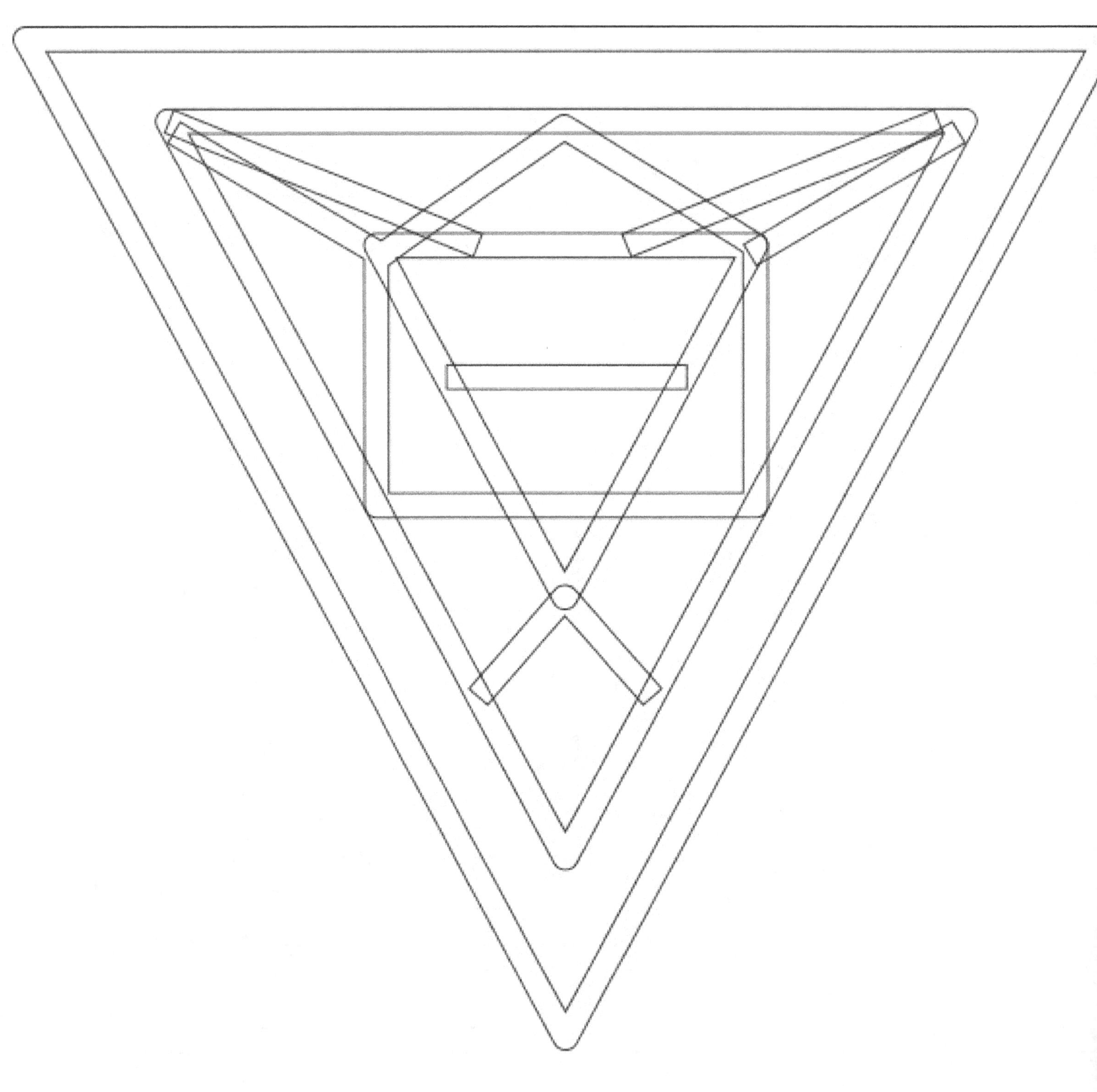

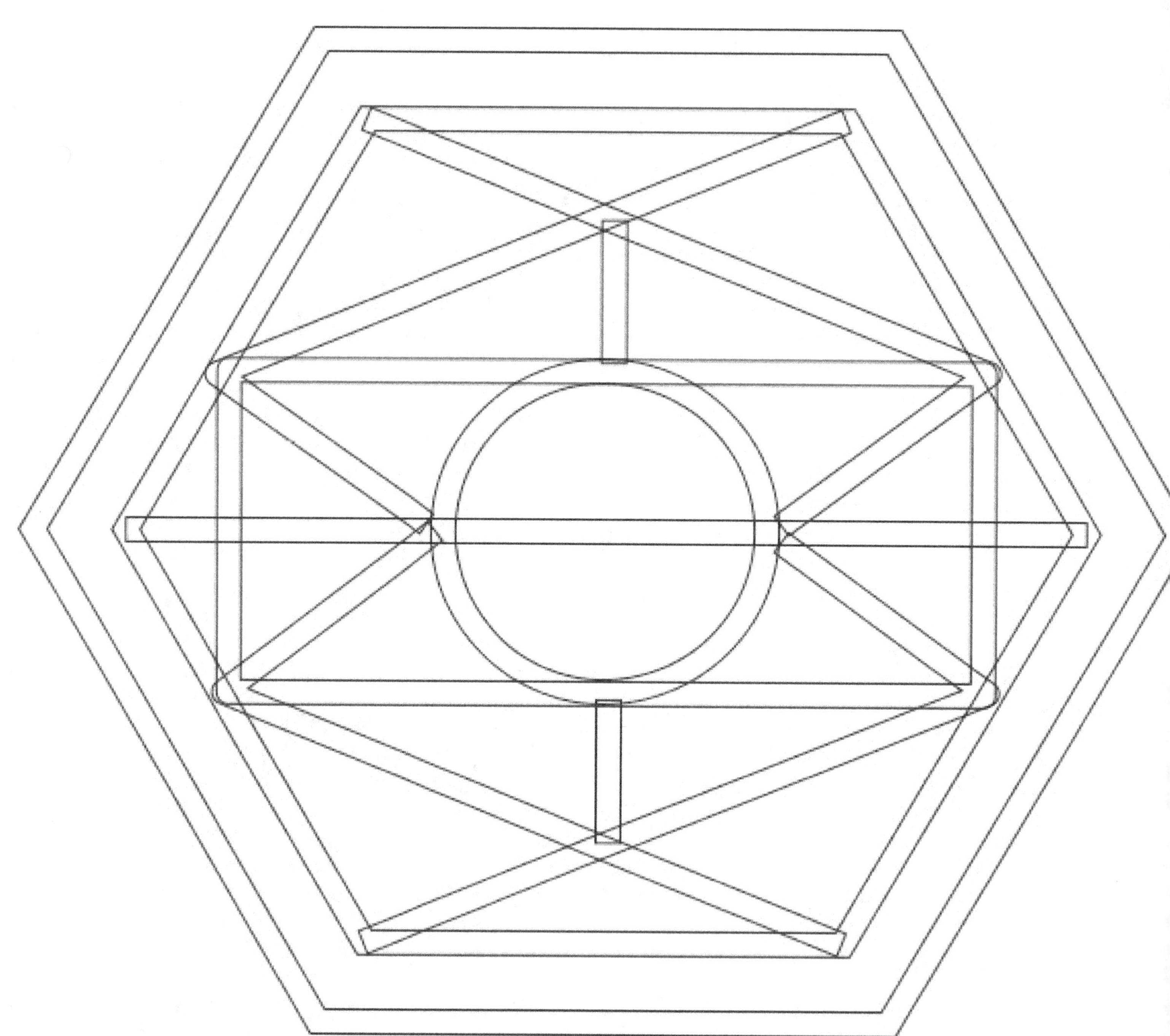

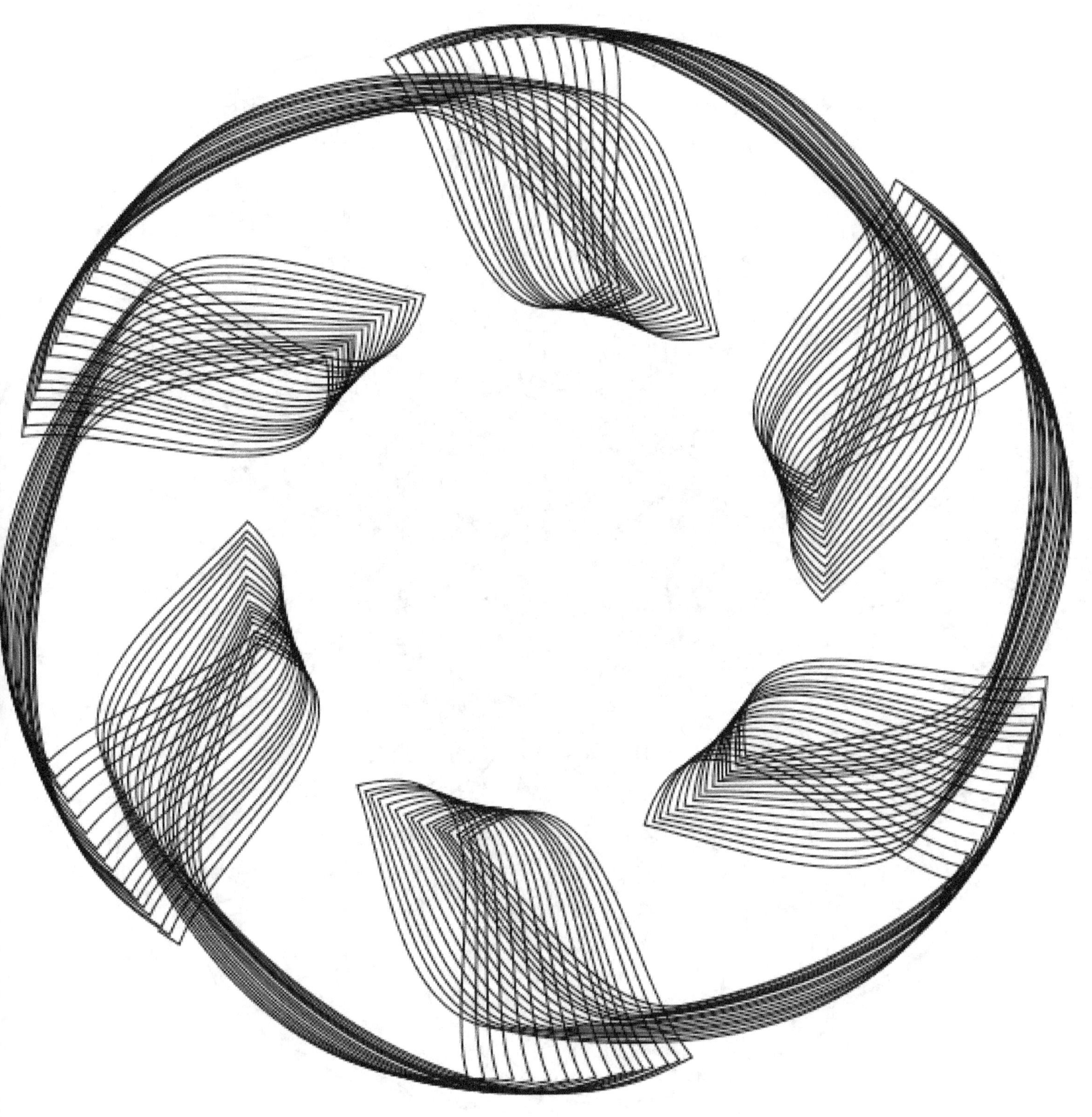

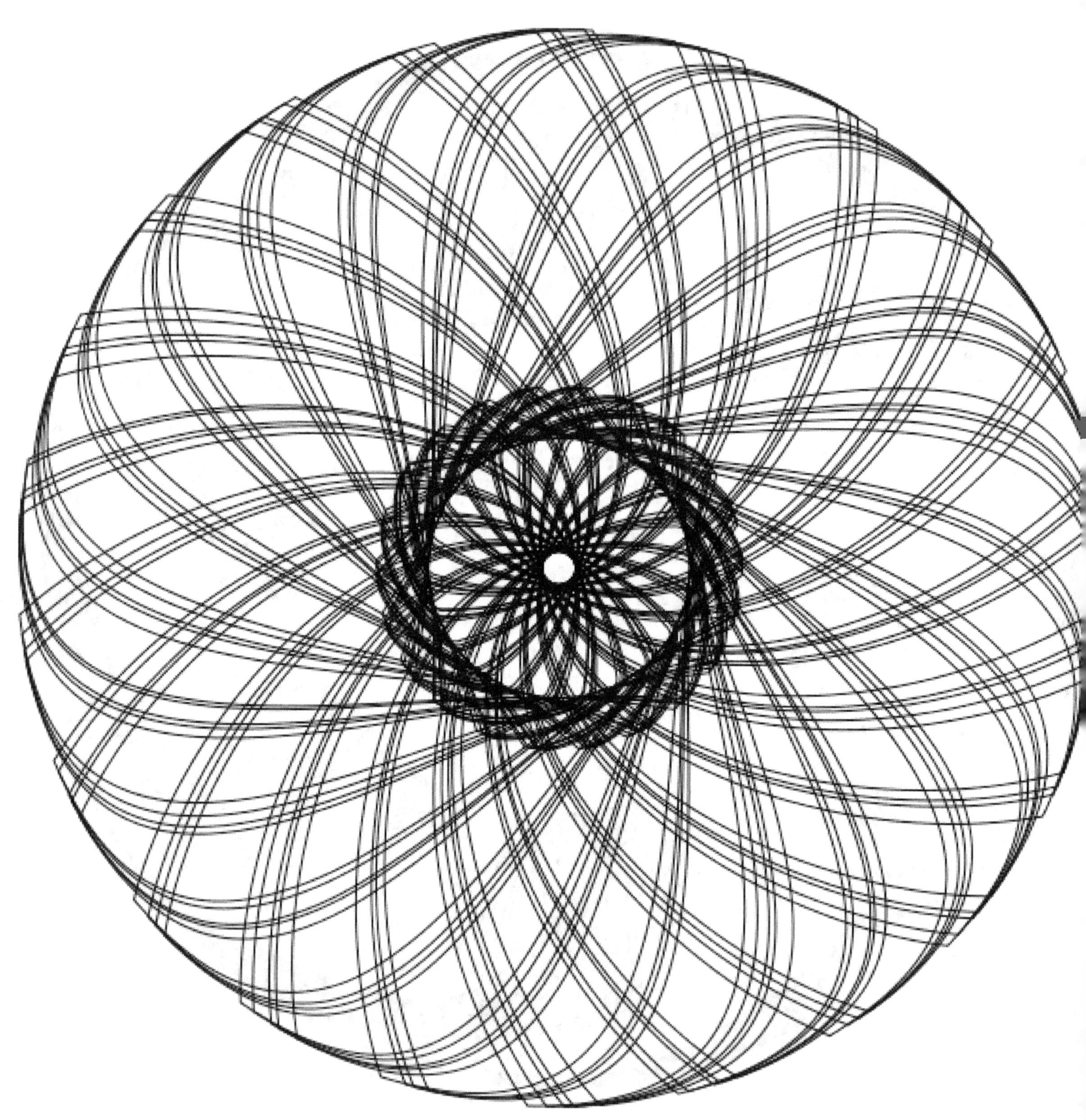

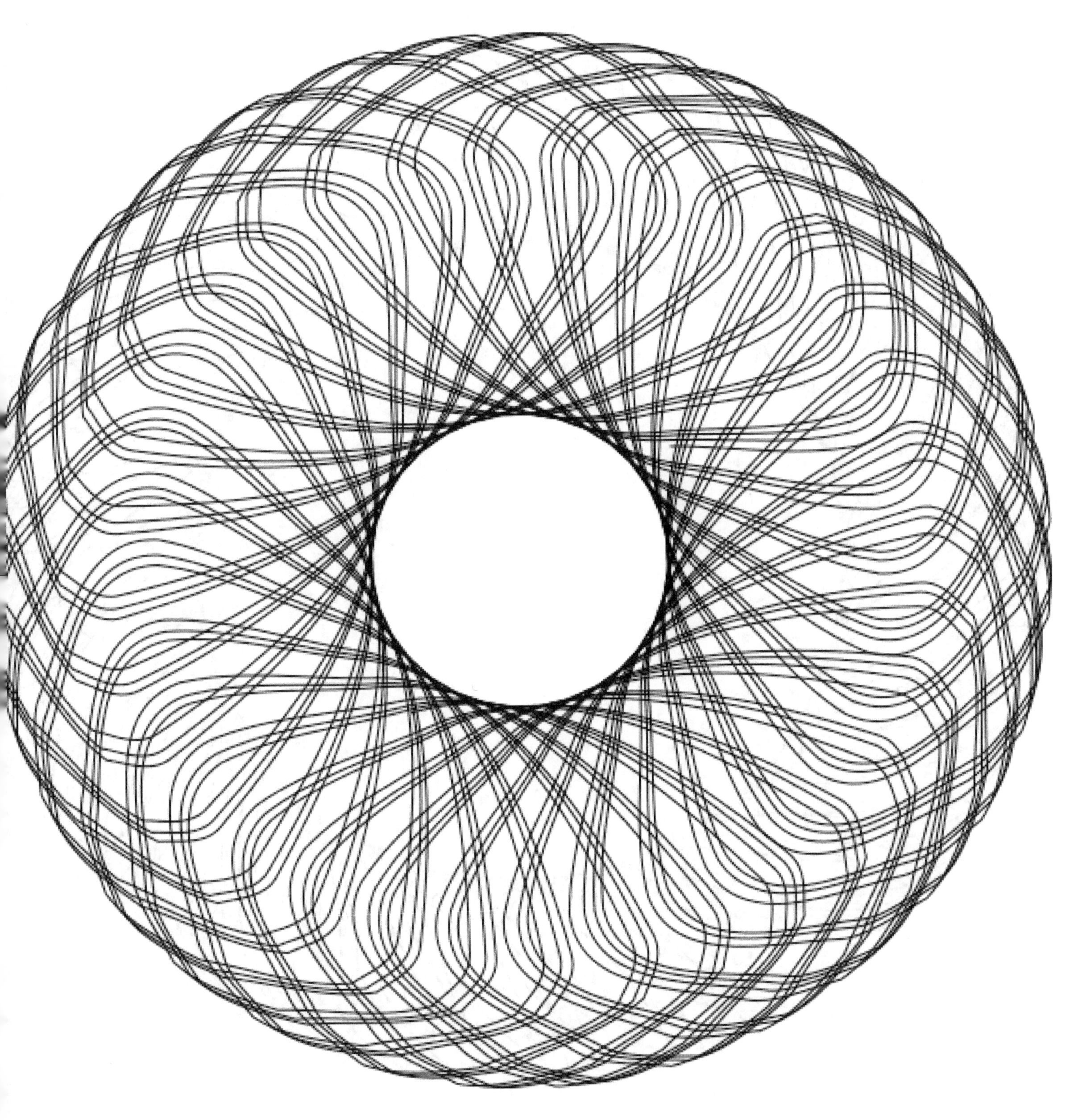

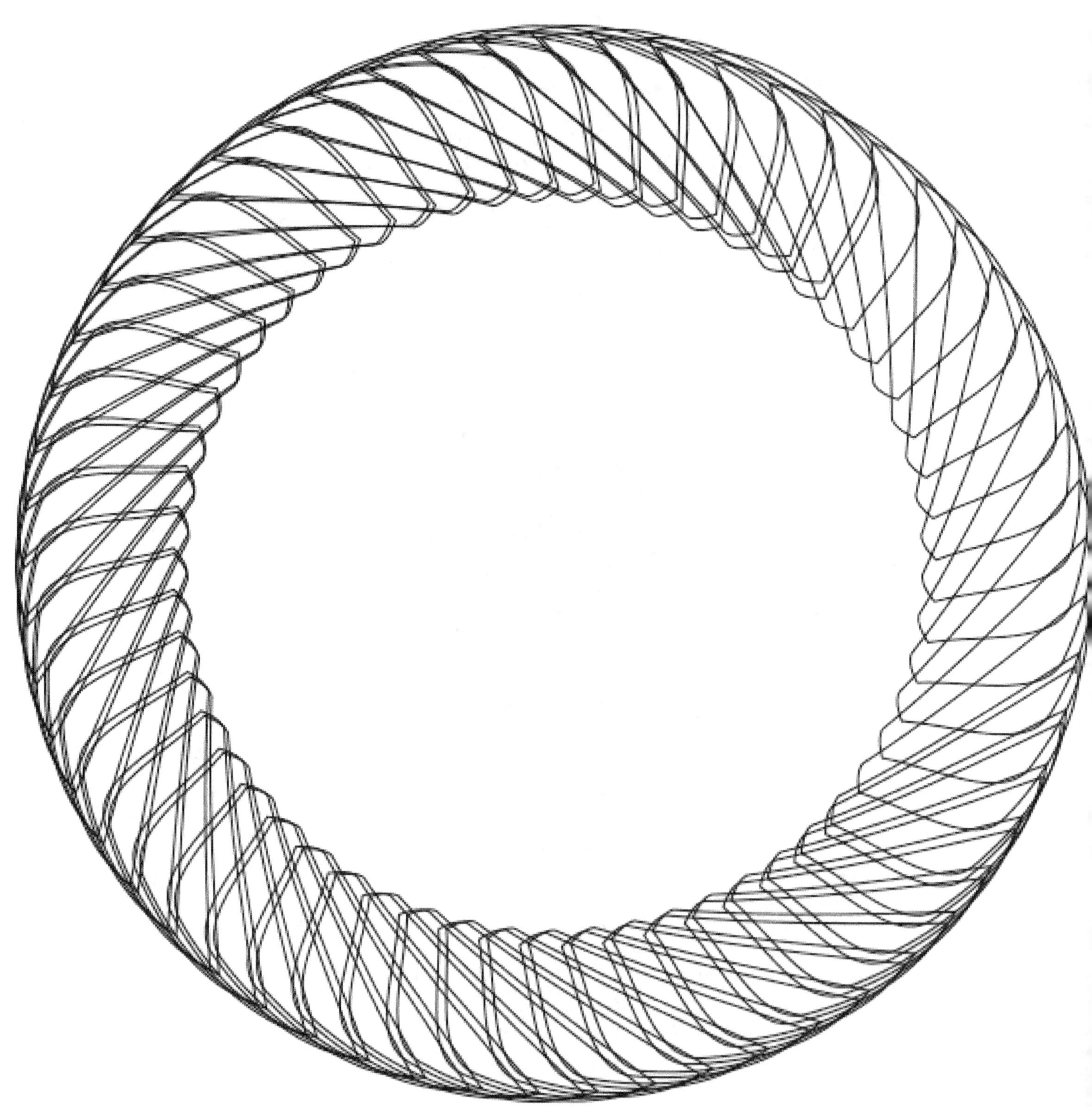

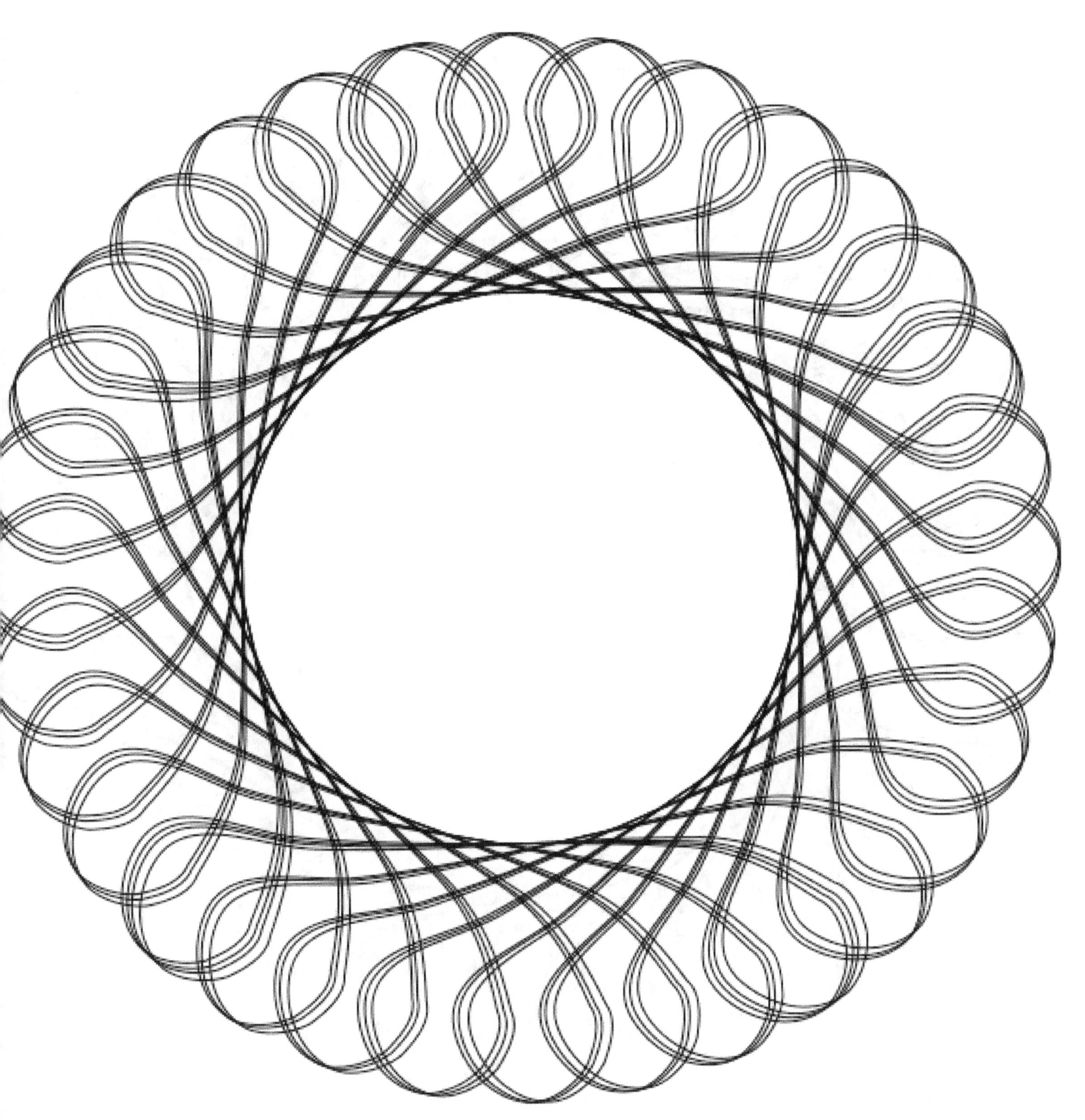

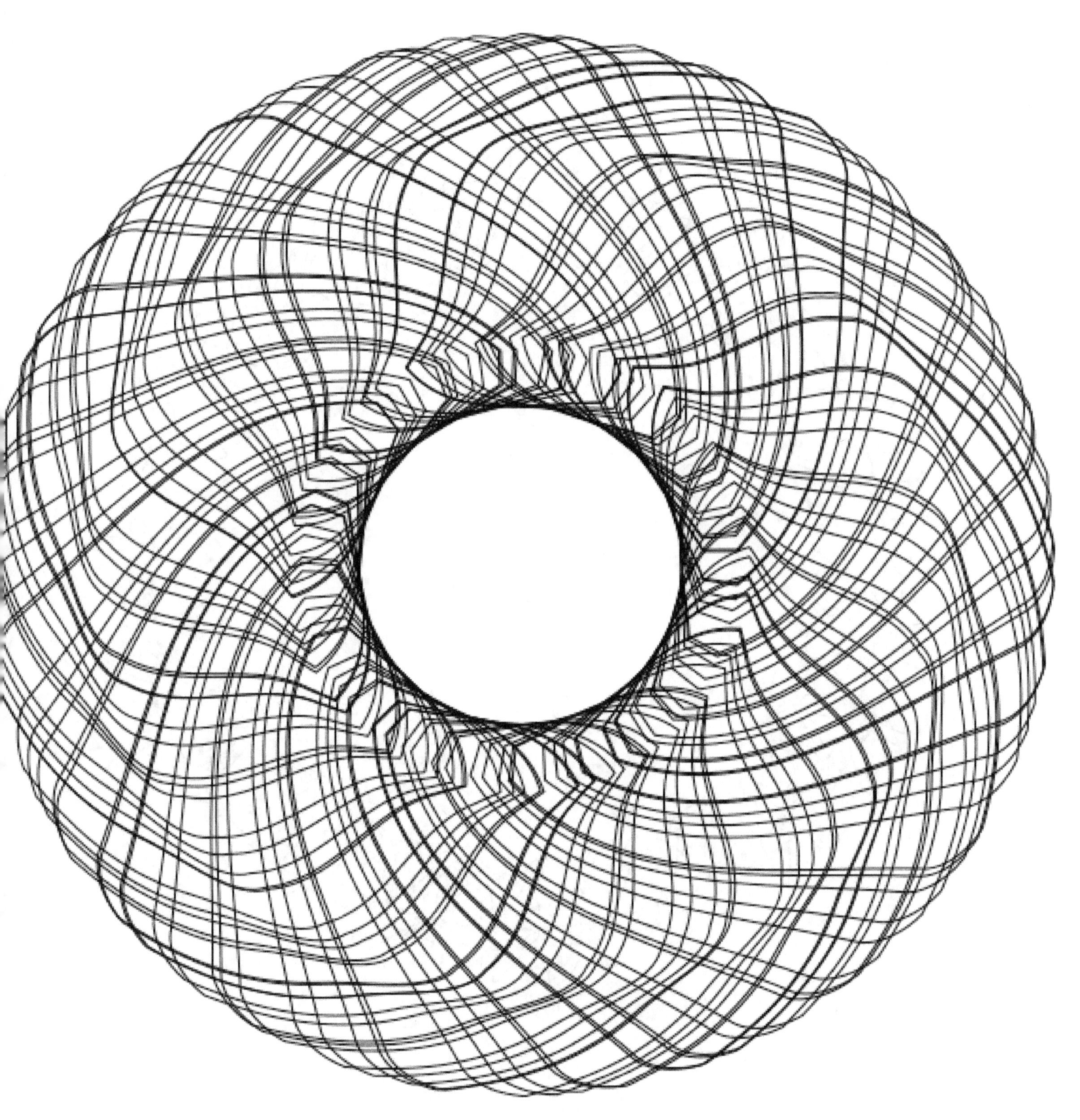

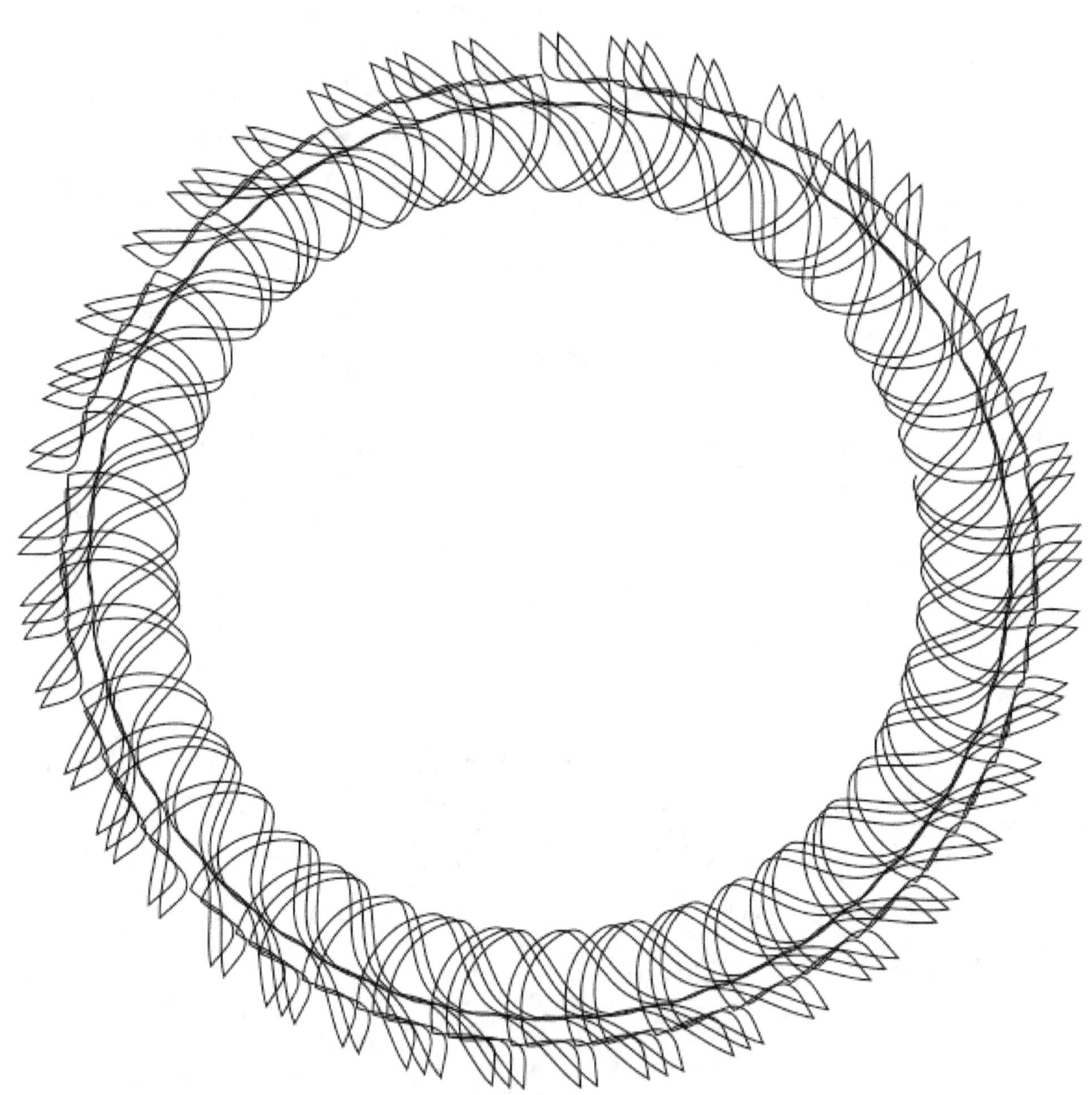

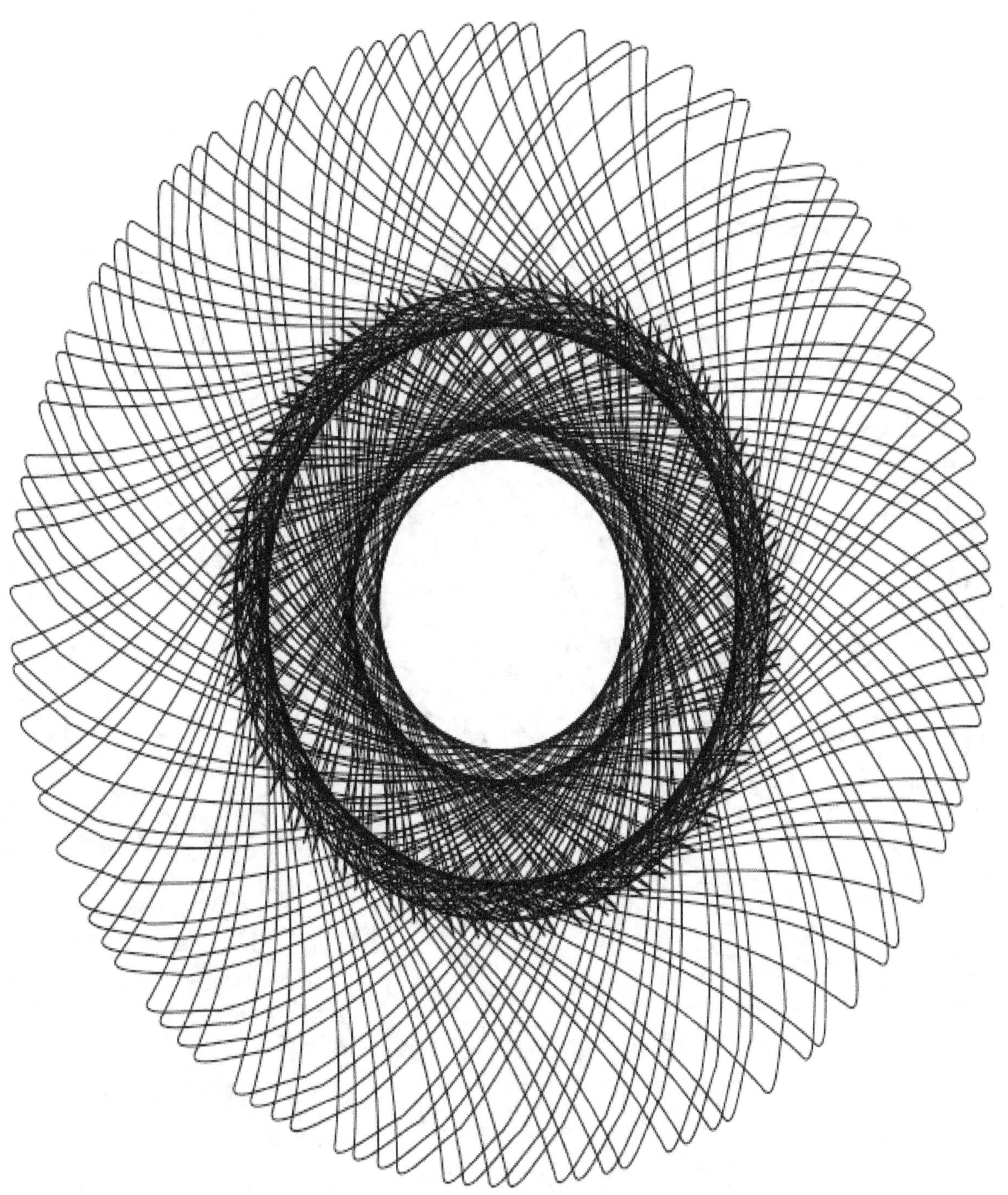

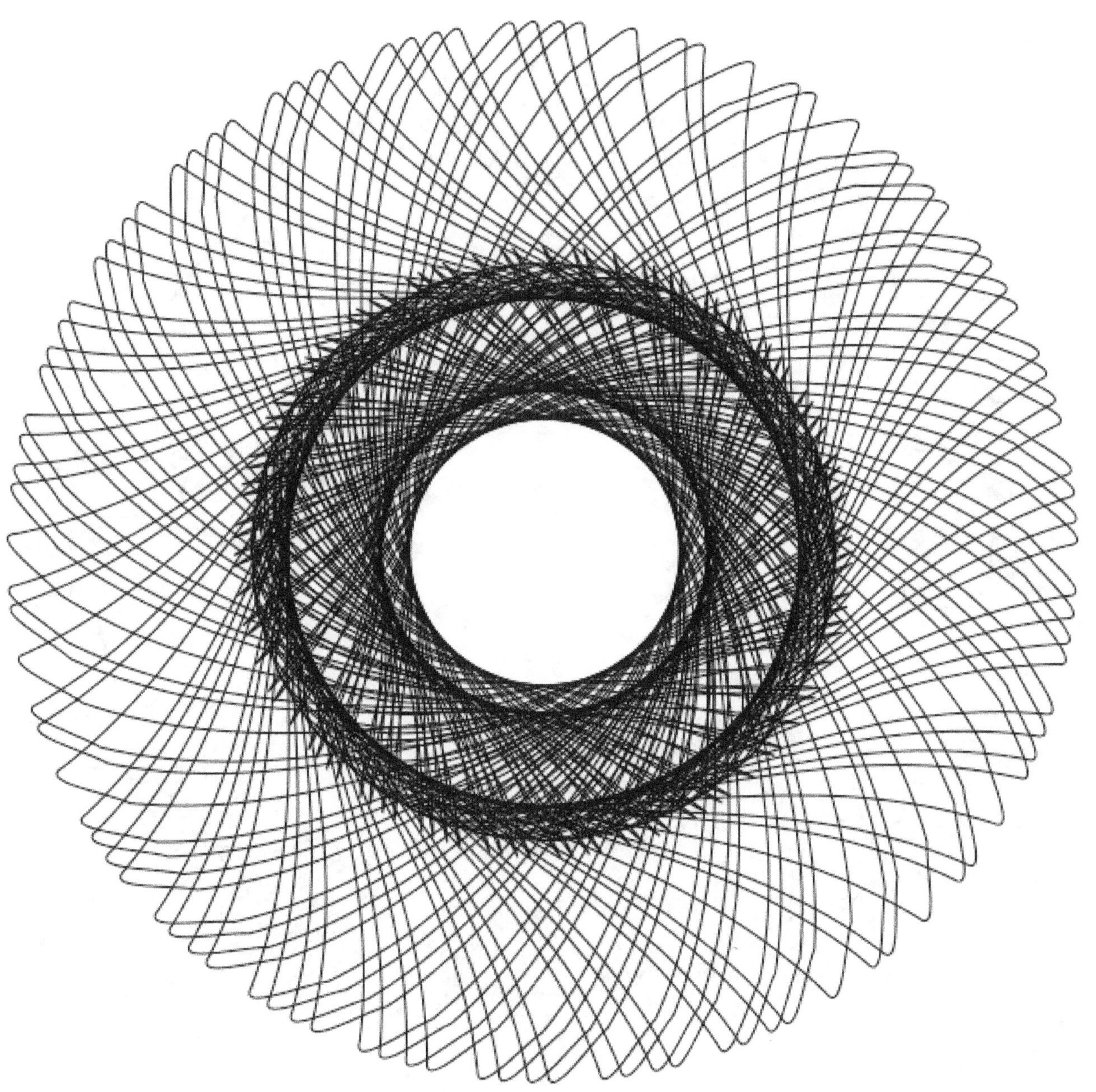

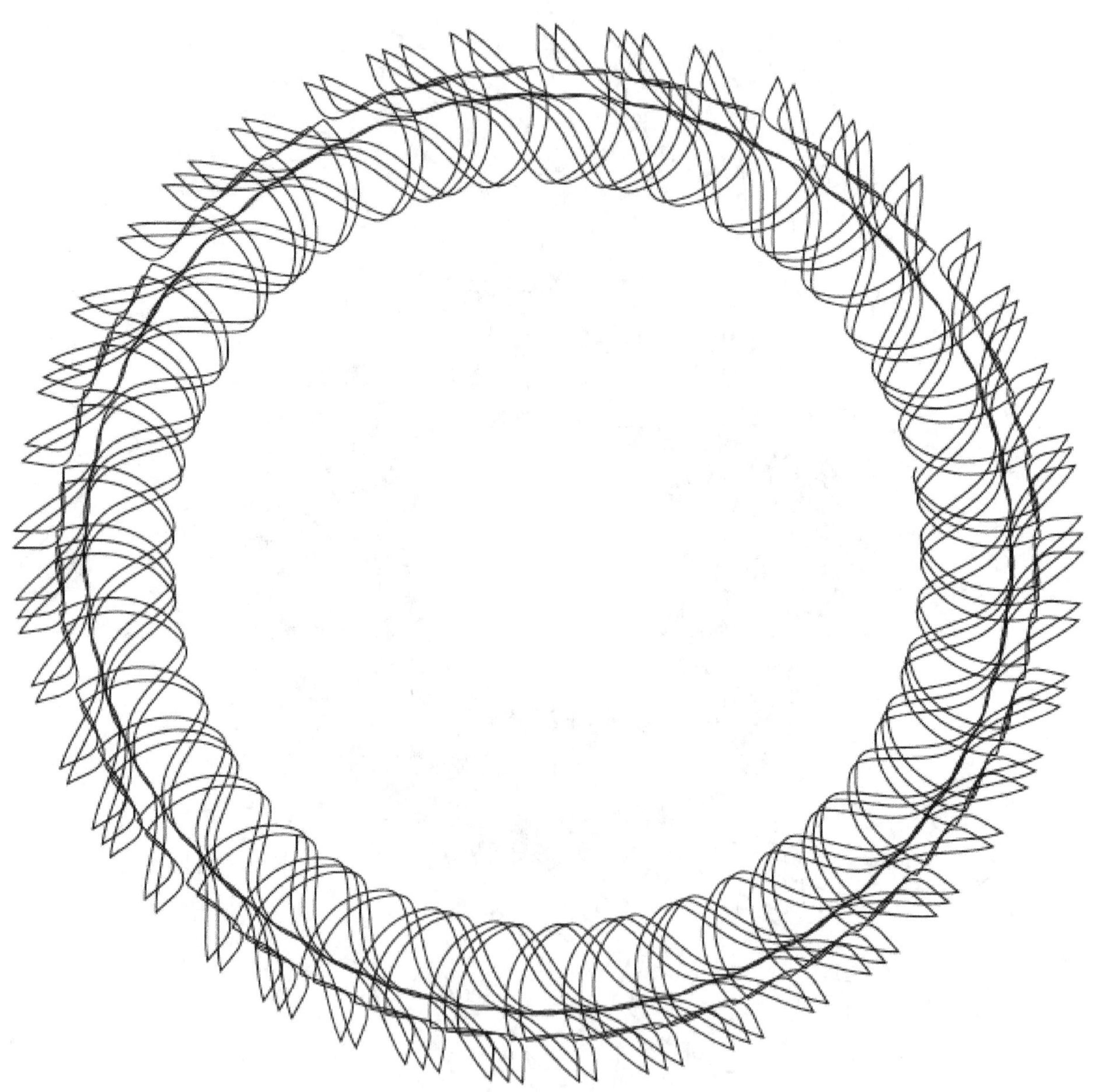